DEANO

Dean Richards

with

Peter Bills

VICTOR GOLLANCZ
LONDON

First published in Great Britain 1995
by Victor Gollancz
An imprint of the Cassell Group
Wellington House, 125 Strand, London WC2R 0BB

A catalogue record for this book is
available from the British Library.

ISBN 0 575 06110 3

Typeset by Rowland Phototypesetting Ltd,
Bury St Edmunds, Suffolk
Printed and bound in Great Britain by
Mackays of Chatham, plc

Contents

Foreword

Strength and reliability are two qualities that we admire constantly in our business. We also have a great admiration for those who do things professionally and to the highest standards, whatever task they seek to achieve. It seemed therefore a natural partnership for CSB Meridian to team up with Dean Richards for his autobiography, *Deano*. Our company, which specializes in computer systems for the clothing and textile trade, has been based in Hinckley, the town where Dean Richards learned his rugby, for five years. In all he does, Dean shows the kind of qualities we admire: he is loyal to those around him in his club, Leicester Tigers; he is quiet and unassuming and gets on with his job whatever the circumstances.

People relate to Dean Richards because he is more than just a reluctant hero. He transcends the gap from ordinary club bloke to international rugby superstar with assured ease, because although he is a great player he is also extremely modest. He has achieved all he has achieved simply because he genuinely enjoys playing rugby.

We have been firm followers of Leicester Tigers for some years now and have always enjoyed watching Dean Richards' contribution to their successes, highlighted by the winning of the Courage Club Champions title last spring at Welford Road. We have also followed Dean's international career closely and believe that our company could not wish to have a liaison with a finer player, one who is respected around the world and yet is so unassuming a man. The combination of the two make

Dean Richards a very special individual. Though quiet in appearance and approach, when Dean Richards plays rugby, whether as captain, pack leader or simply as a source of inspiration, he is in total command. He is totally professional in his play at all times, a trait which we as a growing business wish to emulate every day of our working lives.

CSB Meridian admires Richards, a man whom anyone can relate to, for all he has achieved in his outstanding career. For example, to have reached the landmark of 100 tries for Leicester as a forward even before Rory Underwood, acknowledged as one of the game's greatest try scorers, was quite an extraordinary feat. The story of Dean's career in this revealing and entertaining book will, we are sure, delight rugby followers all over the country and indeed in many other rugby-playing lands. We are proud to have been involved in its production.

Steve Brown
John Norman

Joint Managing Directors,
CSB Meridian Ltd, Hinckley

1 Three World Cups: Exercises in Self-Destruction

I sat in the dressing room, deep in the bowels of Newlands Stadium, Cape Town. The focus of my attention was an irrelevant little mark on the floor. At this moment, it was as good a thing to study as anything else. Outside, in the stadium, New Zealanders were celebrating their team's victory over England in the semi-final of the 1995 World Cup. Here, fifteen weary players, a few reserves and various others pondered our exit from the tournament.

There was one thought flooding through my own mind. I felt that, as in the first World Cup in Australia and New Zealand in 1987, we ourselves had been the chief destroyer of our chances of glory. Then, all those years ago, we had prepared for an important quarter-final against Wales by going paragliding, water-skiing, sunbathing and relaxing on Hamilton Island on the Great Barrier Reef. We lost the match 16–3. Ever since, I have thought that we blundered in taking it easy just a few days before the game. Now, almost exactly the same thing happened again. We had celebrated our quarter-final victory over Australia at Newlands by going off for two days' recreation at Sun City.

When you go to places like Sun City your mind is totally off it. You are not thinking about the match ahead, sitting down studying videos and analysing your opponents. Don't get me wrong – spending hour after hour looking at rugby videos is not something I relish. But when you are about to play New

Zealand for a place in a World Cup final, you have to do whatever is necessary. We didn't do that, and, because of 1987, I knew even in the moments leading up to the semi-final that the trip had been a wrong move.

In 1987, the risks of allowing ourselves to relax hadn't really occurred to me. I was relatively new to international rugby and I just thought it was the done thing. But as a result the England players were not mentally tuned in that day in Brisbane. Wales were more focused than us, and despite some appalling injury problems, they deserved their upset win. It was a day of bitter disappointment for me and everyone else involved in English rugby, yet incredibly, in 1995 we repeated the mistake.

For encounters of the magnitude of World Cup matches – especially a semi-final – the build-up doesn't begin two days earlier. It might take a week, even two weeks sometimes, to get ready both mentally and physically for a really big game. Here in Cape Town, as in Brisbane in 1987, England's players were off the pace because they had been allowed to slacken mentally. OK, this time was slightly different in that we didn't drink, as we had done in the first World Cup, but we were still winding down when we should have been keying it all up for the All Blacks match. Players cannot just turn it on and off like a tap, especially at international level. Consequently, we did not give a true account of ourselves in Cape Town.

I don't think this is a case of being wise after the event, because I was very surprised the management let us go off to Sun City in the first place. Long before we had even left England, I suggested that the ideal way to incorporate some leisure time into the visit would be for the RFU to give us a trip away for a few days *after* our World Cup was over. Even when we got to Sun City, I suggested to Jack Rowell that we ought to fit in a couple of training sessions just to keep our minds on the job ahead – an unusual request coming from me. That too was pooh-poohed.

We had originally intended to stay for just one night but we were told that because we had done so well, we would be staying for two nights. This was just compounding the error. We stayed at a very luxurious, if somewhat ostentatious hotel in Sun City. As I'd had injury problems, I basically just rested, but many of the boys made use of the water sports, golf, casino and so on. And we weren't all tucked up in bed by ten o'clock at night. The boys were given a free rein and some of them went over the top with the holidaying. They let everything go and forgot what they were there for. We didn't get back to Johannesburg until lunchtime on the Wednesday before the big match, and our first training session of the week was later that day, in the early evening at the Wanderers Club. Too late. Too much time had been lost.

Everyone knows the outcome. The match was over after fifteen minutes because New Zealand caught us cold. In fact, after that initial shock I thought we played some good rugby, but you don't come back and beat the All Blacks from 35–3 down without a miracle. So as we sat in that silent dressing room, we had a lot of food for thought. Another doubt which crossed my mind was the wisdom of allowing us to have our wives and girlfriends out in South Africa while the World Cup was going on. Of course, it was great for me to be able to see my wife Nicky and daughter Jessica whenever I could. Yet it became pretty obvious that, even at crucial times, some people's minds were on personal matters when they should have been thinking about nothing but rugby. It also fragmented the team a little. Several of the younger players were going out visiting wives or girlfriends when they should have been staying together as a group. It got to the point where a few of the senior players commented on the situation and Jack Rowell had a word with a couple of the lads about it. England were only one of two countries at the World Cup whose wives and girlfriends were around during the tournament. New Zealand didn't permit it, and rightly so. It is a distraction and it hinders the process of building up that tight-knit feeling of togetherness among the players.

And so, for whatever reasons, the chance to win another World Cup had slipped away. The sobering reality is that this was the third time England had failed in their quest for the World Cup due to their own misjudgements. The first tournament, though, was very much uncharted territory. Even a few weeks before it was due to start, everyone had been wondering whether it would actually go ahead or not. We started off by losing to Australia, somewhat unluckily, since David Campese 'scored' a try which should never have been allowed. We did reach the quarter-finals, but we should have done better. You gain a mental hardness by being involved in a World Cup and had we not let that slip away by going off on holiday in the middle of it all, we could have reached the semi-finals. We wouldn't have beaten New Zealand on that occasion, though. They were a formidable outfit, probably the best prepared of all the countries, and worthy winners. England were captained in 1987 by Michael Harrison, who really started the change in attitude in English rugby. He provided a link between the players and the RFU committee and instigated improvements in the consideration of our wives and girlfriends as well.

If the first World Cup took rugby on to another plateau, the 1991 tournament was a catalyst for the massive development of the game that was to follow. We had prepared much more professionally, going to Lanzarote and Portugal for training trips. We had won the Five Nations that year and were to take it the following year, too – the first back-to-back Grand Slams by any side since England last achieved the feat in 1923 and 1924. So we were on a roll, and we could and should have won that World Cup. I was very disappointed that we didn't. We were naïve enough to get side-tracked into playing a more expansive game than was required against Australia in the final. Before the match we were affected by remarks made by Campo (David Campese) and the other Australian boys, who said we played a very boring game. When we began to prepare for the final, Will Carling, Geoff Cooke and Roger Uttley told us that we could play in a more exciting way and beat Australia in the process. As the day of the game got closer, it became obvious that we were making a colossal error. With two or three days to go, Gary Rees, the Nottingham flanker, and I came away from a training session convinced that it was just not going to work. It was all too apparent that we weren't getting the players over the gain-line.

I know that some of the forwards in the team selected for the final (alas, I was not one of the lucky ones) voiced doubts about whether it was wise to change tactics. The response was that it was a game plan which would work. But we played into the Australians' hands; we lost the psychological battle and eventually we lost the final. We thought we could just switch to a fast, expansive game overnight, but of course that was impossible. If you opt for that open style, the players need constant practice. We should have stuck to the tried and tested formula that had kept us winning and ignored the pre-match banter. In any case, I don't believe England are capable of playing that sort of game. If during that 1991 final we had started to use runners off the side of the scrum, driven through the middle using the forwards as runners and occasionally tried to give the backs an overlap, we would have won it, I am sure of that. We attempted to run too much first-phase possession, and against such a good defence it is very difficult to score that way.

I was, of course, desperately disappointed not to play in that World Cup side from the quarter-final stage onwards, but to watch England virtually play into Australia's hands in the final and in the process throw away their chances of winning the Cup was much worse. The boys on the bench felt we as a team had shot ourselves in the foot. After the time and effort put into our bid for the world title by so many people, it was heartbreaking.

I was told the news that I had been dropped from the side for the quarter-final, against France in Paris, in a hotel corridor. Geoff Cooke came up to me and said: 'I never ever thought I would have to say this to you, but we are going to have to do without you.' I was a little surprised, but I had had an inkling that this might be coming because the backs were always saying they wanted faster forwards. Geoff said he didn't think I was as fast as I could be, but I had played international rugby at that speed for five years and hadn't had too many problems. In fairness to Geoff, I would say that if you live by the sword you must be prepared to die by it too. I wasn't as fit as I could have been, and I've never been very good at training. I hadn't played as well as I might have done in the pool games, and I was disappointed with my performance in the opening match against New Zealand. I was a bit off the pace in that one, although I think everyone was. The tension of the occasion got to us all.

In any case, it would be absurdly arrogant to claim that England would have won the World Cup if I had been playing. That pack was so far superior to any other in the tournament that we should have won it whether I took part or not. But I do think I could have made a contribution in the final. My advice would probably have been to change the game as soon as it became apparent that the new tactics were not working and to bring the play close to me and the forwards. Instead we had been lured into the sort of game plan Australia wanted us to play.

Much had happened in international rugby by the time we set off for South Africa in 1995. And in some respects, the international game now was unrecognizable from that of eight years before, and not just on the field. For a start, we now travelled first class on South African Airways. I spent most of the time playing video golf on the small computer fitted into the back of the seat in front. I also used the time to begin a special diary, which I kept throughout the tour.

Thursday 18 May

Woke at about 6.30 and at 7.20 the plane landed in Johannesburg, where we waited for the connecting flight to Durban. In the departure lounge, I read *Bravo Two Zero*. It was entertaining, a good read. Left for Durban at 10.30 and arrived at the Holiday Inn, North Beach around midday. At 7 p.m. we had our first team meeting to plan for the Argentina match, our opening game, with the help of videos.

Friday 19 May

This morning we met from 9 a.m. to 10 a.m. and then trained at King's Park. The stadium is still not finished, and there is only a week to go before our first game. Because I am not 100 per cent fit, I was in the remedial group, six-packing (doing approximately 150 sit-ups) and watching the others do twenty-five minutes of hard physical training. When the session ended at 1 p.m., Jack Rowell asked me when I would be fit. My leg injury feels better, but I am still four or five days away from full fitness. The heat affects everyone and fluid intake is important. I had more treatment with Smurf (Kevin Murphy, our physio) at 2 p.m. This evening's meeting was taken by Jack, followed by dinner – the food is all high-carbohydrate stuff: pasta, pizza, potatoes etc.

Saturday 20 May

The other boys left the hotel at 7.15 a.m., headed for Cape Town for the official welcoming lunch. I had to stay at the hotel all day with Smurf for more treatment. When I heard about the boys' trip I was glad I hadn't gone. They returned very late, tired and frustrated from so much travelling. They had to travel with three other teams on the same plane, too, which was less than perfect because they didn't want to mix with other teams. To cap it all, there had been torrential rain in Cape Town and the marquee erected for the lunch had sprung a leak and almost collapsed altogether.

Sunday 21 May

This morning we trained at King's Park. My hamstring is feeling much better now and I can run at about 80 per cent speed. The press corps increases by the day and we now have three film crews following us around. No one minds Jim Rosenthal and his crew from ITV – they're familiar with them from the 1991 World Cup. The warm-up was taken by Smurf, followed by a ball-handling session with Les Cosworth for fifteen minutes, and then contact work under Jack's guidance for twenty-five minutes, starting at 50 per cent and then progressing on to full contact. I sat that one out again. The forwards practised rucking and mauling with a small amount of line-out work. Afterwards, Jack asked me again when I would be fit. I'm still not quite there. Generally, the boys are raring to go, and they're all itching to see who will be picked against Argentina. It looks likely to be the team which played Scotland in March, with the exception of Kyran Bracken (Dewi Morris is the favourite at scrum-half) and me.

In the evening, we went for a barbecue at the Durban Deep Sea Fishing Club. It was an idyllic location, with great surf, and the food included fresh oysters just brought in by the divers. Every day we nominate a 'Dick of the Day', who has to wear an outfit consisting of a cowboy-type denim shirt which has a pattern of three cowboys riding across some mountains on the front, plus a hat and belt containing a toy gun. It causes some concern in the streets here! Today the doctor was the winner when he was caught drinking wine from a Coke can.

Monday 22 May

A planned deep-sea fishing trip was cancelled today because we had two training sessions. This morning I felt comfortable after the warm-up so I decided to join in the physical contact work. Suddenly, I pulled up short – the hamstring had pulled again. I sat around for the rest of the session with an ice pack strapped to my leg and feeling desperate. I had more treatment at the hotel in the afternoon, and yet another session after the late-afternoon training, but I am now getting seriously concerned.

Tuesday 23 May

The expected team for the first match was announced to the squad at this morning's training session. It seems as though everyone is overdosing on Rugby World Cup '95 and that nothing else in the world exists. I had a quiet evening, taking a walk along the beachfront before going back for more work on my leg. I'm fed up with this injury and I just want to get out there and play.

Wednesday 24 May

This evening we went to the Sports Café for a meal, which turned out to be a mistake. It was the night of the European Cup final and the place was heaving with drunken Dutch soccer fans celebrating Ajax Amsterdam's win over AC Milan in the final. They were singing and dancing, and leaning on our chairs while we waited for what seemed like ages for our meal. When it finally turned up, we ate it as quickly as possible and left.

Thursday 25 May

I had a lazy morning and then settled down to watch the opening ceremony and the first match, South Africa against Australia. Everybody was staggered by the spectacle of the whole occasion, and by the speed of the game and the big tackles. We all noticed how the shape of the South African players has changed since last summer, when we toured here. They now have generally larger upper bodies. South Africa beat the favourites, Australia, by 27–18. After the game it was back to King's Park for our evening training. The weather was considerably cooler. It was all a bit chaotic and distracting; despite the fact that this was supposed to be a closed session, people were watching from boxes and there was a disco going on in one corner of the ground.

Friday 26 May

This morning it was a captain's session, at which Will went through tactics and set moves or patterns. Then we went out to train for a maximum of forty-five minutes, including warm-ups. In the afternoon we went to Phoenix Township to hold a coaching clinic. Although Phoenix is a predominantly Asian area, we saw participants of all races who showed good enthusiasm and some great skills. It was a real pleasure. My lasting memory of this event will be not only of the children but the singing of the teachers too. They all had lovely voices and sang for us out on the pitch. The players are geared up for the game tomorrow and generally there is a good feeling in the camp.

Saturday 27 May

We left for King's Park at 3.15 p.m., which meant we arrived far too early and had to wait around for ages before our match against Argentina. It was drizzling – not ideal conditions. Nor was it a convincing win (24–18 and a 2–0 try count in the Pumas' favour). All the players were dissatisfied with their performances. During the game I sat in a box with Nicky and Jessica, who arrived this morning, but I should have been with the boys in the squad.

Sunday 28 May

After a 9.30 meeting at the Sports and Racquet Club, where there is a swimming pool and gymnasium, for recuperation and a weights session for me, most of the squad went to Durban Greyville Races. Nicky, Jessica and I, along with Jerry Guscott, his wife Jayne and their two children, spent the afternoon relaxing at a barbecue with some friends who live in Umghlanga, about twenty minutes outside Durban.

Monday 29 May

I spent the morning playing golf at the Royal Durban Course but I lost count of the number of strokes I took. There was time to see Nicky and Jessica briefly in the afternoon before the 5 p.m. training session. I am still only 80 per cent fit. Jack said that he would give me until the Western Samoa game, our final pool match, six days away. It was an ultimatum, all right, but frankly I am relieved to have been given that long. I have been continually telling him I will be fit within three or four days, but it has just gone on and on.

Tuesday 30 May

The captain's session for the game against Italy tomorrow was taken by Rob Andrew as Will is injured. The players are quite tense. They know they did not perform well in the first game and that places are up for grabs. Not in my case, though. I had a lazy afternoon and walked along the seafront worrying about my hamstring injury.

Wednesday 31 May

Match day against Italy. Our performance was again far from convincing, even though we got a 27–20 win. There were too many errors and we gave away easy tries; a lack of conviction, concentration and effort. Something is wrong, but I can't put my finger on it. The backs and forwards seem to be working as two separate units rather than as a team. As for me, it was back to the treatment table after the match before having a few beers in the evening.

Thursday 1 June

As there were a few bumps and bruises after last night's game, we decided to go for some rest and recuperation at the Sports and Racquet Club, as we did after the Argentina game. In the afternoon we went paint-balling, a devious little game I invented in which you use toy guns to fire little balls full of paint. It is very painful when they hit you because they are pressurized by gas. We played forwards against the backs, a real war. Before we even started, Jerry, who mistakenly thought his gun wasn't loaded, was going round firing at people. Martin Johnson got a couple of direct hits and a couple of nice bruises before Jerry realized what he'd done. The forwards beat the backs quite decisively, even though Kyran was shooting people in the supposedly neutral territory of the reloading bay. In the evening, we went to the Durban Country Club where we met our wives for a cocktail party. Jayne and Nicky were a bit late arriving as they had to put the girls to bed, so Jerry and I had a game of snooker.

Friday 2 June

Tonight's training was meant to be a closed session, but we were watched by several people. Some of them appeared to be trying to hide, so it was very off-putting. Jack (Rowell) held one of his mess-around sessions, the intention of which seems to be to get us to make as many mistakes as possible in order to keep us on our toes. He thinks we sometimes get a little too confident and wants to bring us down to earth. I think he's right about that, but sometimes on this trip he does it at the wrong time. In the end we took most of the session ourselves and it didn't turn out too badly. The team which has been selected to play Western Samoa is totally different, with Mike Catt at fly-half, Jon Callard at full-back, Ian Hunter on the wing, Phil de Glanville at centre, Graham Dawe at hooker, Richard West in the second row and Graham Rowntree at prop. The back row is to be Backy (Neil Back), Oj (Steve Ojomoh) and me – a game at last. The introduction of these players has given the squad something to aim at and we all worked extremely hard to try to improve our performance.

Saturday 3 June

The captain's session this morning took longer than usual, because we had to work out things for a different side. The day seemed to drag: there was a lot of hanging around, especially for the new boys. Damian Hopley and John Mallett are to be on the bench and look like being the only members of the squad who won't win a cap. We all felt quite sorry for them, but at the same time, we are here to win the World Cup, and the best team, in the view of the selectors, has to be chosen.

Sunday 4 June

Our last Pool Match against Western Samoa was a late kick-off, 8 p.m. At last we won fairly convincingly, by 44–22, but in the process we suffered several injuries which resulted in Brian Moore and Kyran Bracken having to pack down as wing forwards before the end! The side was full of fairly inexperienced players with a point to prove, and many of them put in very good performances. Neil Back had an outsanding game; Graham Rowntree did very well and the back line was extremely swift and decisive in everything they did with Mike Catt at fly-half.

The game also saw both Damian Hopley and John Mallett take the pitch as replacements for Will and Graham Rowntree, so they got their caps after all, and well deserved they were too – both players gave a very good account of themselves. It is difficult to pinpoint why, but we all played with a lot more fire and spirit than we had in either of the other two games and it seemed to boost the morale of the whole squad.

So we have won our group, and will meet Australia, the second-placed team in Pool A, in the quarter-finals. I don't think we should allow our success against Western Samoa to influence selections for the Australia game, but if we can overcome the Aussies and meet New Zealand in the semis, as seems likely, I think we should pick horses for courses for that match. It might even be an idea to bring in Neil Back if we play New Zealand, because they have a fast, genuine openside flanker in John Kronfeld who we would need to match. I would not be happy to be left out for him, but I would accept it.

Monday 5 June

No training today – instead we left for Johannesburg after quite a quiet night. By the time the match ended, it seemed too late to do very much. We are staying at the Sunnyside Park Hotel in Jo'burg – and so are the Western Samoans, which came as something of a shock. In theory, we might meet them again in the tournament – in the final. You don't put two teams in the same hotel when that is a possibility, however remote. We also discovered what the initial arrangements had been for next weekend's game against Australia. Originally we were to fly down to Cape Town on the evening before the game and back to Johannesburg straight afterwards on the Sunday evening. Representations were made in the hope of getting these arrangements changed and eventually we were successful. Now we will arrive earlier, on the Friday, and leave the day afterwards, which gives us a slightly longer breathing space.

Tuesday 6 June

I had a long lie-in today – until 9 a.m.! Jeff Miller, the former Wallaby flanker, with whom I've always got on well, rang from Australia. He wanted me to get a shirt signed for him. He told me he'd been in touch with the Australian boys and they felt things were going well for them in training. It was nice to hear what was going on. We met for training ourselves at 10 a.m. at the University Ground, another immaculate pitch. We did a warm-up, missed rhythms and then played five-a-side with Les, the doctor, Dave Alred, the kicking coach, Victor Ubogu and J.C. There were four teams, and mine came last! It did get rather heated: Will was heavily tackled by Brian Moore and lashed out with his feet, and Catty tackled Johnno 20 yards from the ball. But it was a bit of light relief away from serious training, and I think we all enjoyed it. Perhaps we should have done this a bit more, because training has been a bit tedious at times. You can make it too intense over a six-week period; sometimes you need a less serious approach just for some variety. Otherwise it is very monotonous – virtually the same routines day in day out – and it's hard to make it interesting all the time.

In the afternoon, went on a trip to the Sandton Shopping Mall. I found a great gun and knife shop where a man bought a pistol for 150 rand (approximately thirty pounds). After our 6 p.m. team meeting Jack gave a brief talk, and after dinner I played pool with Kyran, Jerry, Richard and Hunts while the others went to watch Mike and the Mechanics in concert. I had some acupuncture at 10.15 and then I went to bed.

Wednesday 7 June

Today it was straight back to serious training for me, even though I have a stiff neck from the Western Samoa game and my hamstring is also still playing up. I decided I wanted to take a full part anyway – there aren't too many World Cup quarter-finals in your career, and I am desperate to play and to win. The only way I can do that is to play through the problems. All credit to Smurf and the doctor – they have both worked really hard on my neck and hamstring and it has paid off, even if I couldn't truthfully say I'm 100 per cent fit.

Thursday 8 June

We went paintballing again, and it turned into something of a bloodbath. Backy finished up with about ten shots (and consequently bruises) on his buttocks and an equal number on his back, mainly from Kyran and Phil. Several other people also came away a bit bruised.

Our training is becoming more and more focused, but we have heard rumours that, should we win against Australia, we will be going to Sun City after the match as a sort of reward. Everyone is trying to put these thoughts aside for now, though – we have to beat Australia first. The usual taunts from David Campese about our style of play have started. It is not unusual for Bob Dwyer then to chip in as well. We had a chat about Australia and how boring they are and discussed our game plan, which we have decided to keep as it is as we felt we could beat them that way.

Friday 9 June

We trained in the morning at the local police ground and went straight from there to the airport for our flight to Cape Town.

Saturday 10 June

The captain's session was held at Newlands in the morning. The pitch was quite damp and spongey, and after half an hour we felt that it would be taking quite a lot out of our legs to train for much longer, so we finished early. It had been raining non-stop before we arrived and was still quite windy, although earlier in the morning there had been brilliant sunshine.

In the afternoon I met Nicky and Jessica at the Waterfront, a very pleasant new development of shops, restaurants and hotels right beside the harbour, just for an hour. It was a bit of a break.

The evening meeting was a bit out of the ordinary. Jack made his usual speech about us having to win and so on, and then Austin Swain, the sports psychologist from Loughborough University, took over. He did something I have never come across before. He got each of us to write something constructive about every one of the other members of the squad, collected the pieces of paper and put the comments on each player in a separate envelope. I must admit that it really isn't my cup of tea, but I know that it works for some people. I took part, however, although some of my comments were probably not quite what the boys wanted to hear. I had a bit of a laugh with Jerry and some of the Leicester boys. I was given an envelope with twenty-one pieces of paper in. I read the first couple and then I threw the rest in the bin – I don't need things like that to motivate me. However, I do appreciate that it does work for others and it may be worth trying at Leicester to see whether it is successful there.

After the meeting, I had a game of cards, and by the end of the evening I was a couple of hundred rand up.

Sunday 11 June

Everybody will remember the 25–22 result of our quarter-final against Australia since we won it in the closing moments with that injury-time dropped goal from Rob. It was a great game, played at pace, with both sides fully committed. Tony Underwood scored a cracking try. There were fantastic scenes of jubilation in the changing room afterwards. Everybody was very emotional – some players were even crying. As for me, I just went and sat in a jacuzzi in another dressing room on my own and had a quiet soak for twenty minutes to let it all sink in. I'd seen it all before, and we now have to take stock of the situation and look towards next week. We all realized that it is going to be very hard to raise our game again for the semi-final in such a short space of time. Perhaps we let our emotions run away with us a bit. Our wives are leaving tomorrow, so we went out for the evening with them.

Monday 12 June
Rest and recreation in Sun City. It's been a good couple of days, but the timing was wrong – we should have gone there when our World Cup ends.

Wednesday 14 June
We drove back to Johannesburg this morning and trained in the late afternoon and early evening at the Wanderers Club. Again, this was supposed to be a closed session, but this time there were several cars parked in the road which runs alongside the pitch. Their occupants were furiously scribbling notes. It was just another distraction you don't need.

I got a lot of stick from Jack today for my performance against Australia and we ended up having a fairly heated exchange. He thinks I played badly; I certainly don't claim it was one of my better games, but I am the sort of person who knows when he hasn't played well and doesn't need to be told. Jack just went on about it too much and it niggled me. Of course I will accept being told once, but I don't need someone to keep repeating the point. And he has the habit of doing it in front of others, which I don't like.

Thursday 15 June
Thankfully I had no more stick at training this morning. Perhaps yesterday's spat has cleared the air. More serious is the fact that I'm still suffering with my shoulder, which is bruised down to the elbow as a result of a tackle I made in the quarter-final. The doctor and physio are working hard on it.

Friday 16 June
After training early this morning we flew back to Cape Town, where we will meet New Zealand on Sunday. This time we are

staying at the Holiday Inn Garden Court on Eastern Boulevard, where we were mobbed by supporters when we arrived. The rooms are not as good as previous ones but are adequate. When the evening meeting finished we went to the cinema to see *Bad Boys*, which was awful.

Saturday 17 June

This morning's captain's session at Newlands went reasonably well. In the afternoon I had a sleep and then watched half of the other semi-final, between South Africa and France. It was quite tense: Durban was hit by incredible storms and the start was delayed for an hour and a half, so the conditions were absolutely awful. France were unlucky to have lost, but on the day I think South Africa had the edge.

The evening meeting was fairly quiet – there was no psychological stuff like the exercise we'd done before the Australia game, but Austin Swain was there and he did suggest that we reread the notes our team-mates had written about us. Unfortunately, mine were in a wastepaper bin somewhere in Cape Town. I sensed a feeling that we weren't clued up as much for this game as we had been before the quarter-final, and I'm sure this is due to the effects of our unwinding in Sun City – we've had just three and a half days to try to build it all up again.

Sunday 18 June

Well, the semi-final turned out to be a game of fifteen minutes. After that stage, New Zealand were out of sight and we were out of the World Cup. Normally, the opening part of the match is fairly equal; both sides tend to be very keyed up and they neutralize one another. Unfortunately, in this case it was all over by the time we had got into our stride, and all we could do was play catch-up rugby. Everything went their way – the bounce of the ball, Zinzan Brooke's dropped goal, everything. After the initial onslaught we did in fact start to play some good rugby, but by then we were so far behind that we were having to take risks. The final score was 45–29.

After the game we sat down and discussed it, but everyone was so shell-shocked that they seemed to forget that we had actually played some good rugby. Yet the inescapable fact was that we had blown everything in that first quarter of an hour, because, I felt, we weren't focused enough. I sat down with Jerry and we both agreed that we hoped there would be no finger-pointing by any of the players. While it is true that the idea of bringing in someone special to mark Jonah Lomu, New Zealand's secret weapon, was discussed, it had been ruled out pretty quickly. And besides, it wasn't only Tony Underwood who missed tackles on Lomu. We sat around in the dressing room for twenty-five minutes before anyone could even think about moving. But once we had started to come to terms with the situation I thought to myself, we still have a big game to play on Thursday and we need to start recovering mentally from this as quickly as possible.

We then had to suffer the indignity of having to travel back to Johannesburg on the same flight as the All Blacks, the New Zealanders in first class and us in economy. That really set the seal on our day. In Jo'burg all the bars were shut, so we went to the Sports Café. It was very quiet: there were only about ten people in there. We just sat there pondering our futures over a few beers.

Monday 19 June

Today was a rest day. Everybody was still down. We went to the Sports and Racquet Club in the morning and then travelled to Pretoria, where we are due to meet France in the third-fourth-place play-off match. We checked into the same hotel that the New Zealanders had just left. In the evening we went to the cinema.

Tuesday 20 June

At breakfast, Jack asked me how my shoulder was. It was still a little sore, but I told him I would be available for the play-off match. Nevertheless he decided, without seeking the opinion of either the physio or doctor, as far as I know, that I wouldn't be. I felt he just wanted me out of the side for the France match. That would've been OK with me if he'd wanted to counter the speed of Laurent Cabannes by playing someone really quick in the back row, Neil Back, for example. As I've said, I felt he deserved another chance. But Back was left out as well. In the evening, I met the French players Marc Cecillon and Louis Armary in a bar. They were in the same position as me, so we had a few drinks together and discussed politics and religion. My grasp of French came in useful. In fact, since the World Cup was now over for all of us, we had quite a few drinks – until 6 a.m.

Wednesday 21 June

Training at 9 a.m. went remarkably well, considering that I was extremely hung over. It is very difficult to train with a hangover, but I carried on as normal because I didn't want anyone to know what time I'd got in. I didn't think it would be good for squad morale. The team was announced for the match, and in my view it was the wrong one – not just because I was out, but because I think we should be bringing in younger players who want to prove themselves. The play-off would be a great chance to blood these players.

Thursday 22 June

Everybody in the whole squad was disheartened by the performance against France. It was our most disappointing game of the whole tournament. There was no atmosphere, no passion. I watched it in a box alongside Damian Hopley, John Mallett, Louis Armary and Marc Cecillon, and we were all nonplussed by the occasion.

The evening's court session brought a lot of light relief. Jack and Les were fined for working 'like the locals' and had to wear bib and braces and leather flat caps. The doctor was fined for impersonating a doctor and for prescribing such wonderful cures as mentholyptus for earache. As his punishment he had to wear an outfit like the one worn by the doctor in *Star Trek*. As Will is on the telephone all the time he was sentenced to drag around a Direct Line phone on little wheels all evening.

Friday 23 June

We made our second trip to Sun City, and this time relaxing here was not going to cost us anything, so I drank cocktails most of the day and went to the casino in the evening. Jason Leonard, Damian, Jerry and myself did very well. We won about £3,500 between us on the roulette wheel, and Jerry and I picked up another thousand rand each. We had a late-night drink in the staff bar to celebrate.

Saturday 24 June

World Cup final day, the climax of the tournament. But for us it was awful to have to sit there and watch the match between South Africa and the All Blacks, wishing we had got through but knowing that we didn't deserve to be there. The result, 15–12 to South Africa, achieved only through an injury-time dropped goal from Joel Stransky, was an upset because, yes, New Zealand had brought more to the World Cup, but it's no good playing open rugby and then losing in the final to a side playing orthodox stuff. It was, however, a great day for world rugby, marred only by the after-match-dinner speech from SARFU president Louis Luyt, which was an absolute disgrace. It was three hours from our time of arrival at the dinner before the first course was served, and in the meantime we had to listen to this bigoted speech about the South Africans being the only true world champions and so on. As everyone knows, Louis Luyt claimed that not only were the Springboks world champions now, but they would have won the 1987 and 1991 World Cups as well had they participated. No way was it tongue in cheek, as Luyt was to lamely try to explain days later, after the furore had broken. At the dinner he was deadly serious, and everyone there knew it. He showed no respect for the New Zealanders, and everyone cheered with relief when he sat down.

Even the South African players were shocked and afterwards they apologized for his behaviour. Some penalty should have been imposed on the president by the World Cup organizers for what he said.

Sunday 25 June
I spent the morning packing and paid a visit to the flea market before leaving for the airport and our flight home.

England will win the World Cup one day, perhaps next time, in 1999. But everything has to be right, and it wasn't quite right in 1995. Even against Australia we didn't play brilliantly, but at least we were on the right lines by then. By the end of it all, I wasn't sick of rugby, just very disappointed. The dream was over.

2 The Leicester Family

The legendary sense of humour at Leicester Rugby Club was probably behind the decision to give me my first-team debut for the club against Neath at the Gnoll. Neath, for any readers who might not be steeped in the lore of the game, represents just about as hard a proving ground as it is possible to find in Wales. Visiting any rugby ground in the Principality is a unique experience in sport, but the Gnoll is a cramped, usually tightly packed arena where a particularly tough brand of rugby is invariably served up to the visiting side. It has brought the club its successes, too, although there have been certain incidents in recent years, chiefly against touring teams like New Zealand, Australia and South Africa, which have been less than appealing. So any side visiting Neath knows it will be in for a severe test. In 1982, for an 18-year-old lad with designs on a future in the game at as high a level as possible, it represented a fairly daunting beginning.

This is how Martin Johnson, the Leicester Tigers reporter in those days for the *Leicester Mercury*, previewed the match and my selection:

Dean Richards, an 18-year-old No. 8 who expected to be playing youth rugby this season, makes his debut for Leicester Tigers in the first of their two tough Easter matches in Wales, against Neath at the Gnoll on Saturday. Richards, who gets his chance because of an injury to Angus Collington, played

for England Under-19 Schoolboys at the same time as Barry
Evans, and is highly rated.

Youth team secretary Graham Willars said: 'He's a big lad
with pace, a more than useful line-out jumper and too good
not to be in senior rugby.'

So there, for all those critics who have accused me of not being
able to run, is conclusive proof that 'Deano' was once a positive
gazelle on the field.

The *Mercury* also quoted Chalkie White, Leicester's coach,
who was to be a major influence on me, as saying of me before
that game: 'He is a very fine prospect who is willing to learn.'
I didn't have much option – Chalkie was hardly the kind of
chap you took liberties with!

I'd played only five games in the lower sides, three for the
Swifts and two for the Extras, when I got the news that I had
been selected for the first team. Talk of the Neath match had
been on everybody's lips and it was clear that there was a certain
amount of trepidation among the players. Leicester then was a
very different place from the club today. As was the case at
a lot of English clubs in those days, long before the inception
of the Leagues, people tended to drop out for the hard away
games, but curiously, they could always be relied upon to be
available for the potentially attractive home matches. Now,
with the heavy League programme, we don't have very many
games against Welsh sides, and the League matches against
English clubs are a lot harder. Today, every match in the League
is a pressure game whereas a few years ago there was so much
less at stake. Probably as a consequence of that, people would
suddenly drop out with ailments which became known as
'Gloucester Cough' or 'Neath Knee'.

Nevertheless, in that game we did manage to field quite a
strong side – and against the odds, we won. I was in the back
row with Steve Johnson and Ian Smith, two great servants of
the Leicester club.

You hear a lot about the Welsh being dirty. Well, they were

in those days – notoriously dirty. But you learned to expect it. Before this I'd been playing for Roanne in France for seven or eight months, so I wasn't completely wet behind the ears. You could say I was a little bit more used to the rough and tumble than some lads of eighteen. But this was a different style from French rugby. It was much more organized than anything I had experienced in France and everything was co-ordinated a lot better by the captain and the fly-half. Even so, I hasten to add that I seem to recall being two or three yards behind the pace that day and not quite doing what I should have done. It was a real eye-opener for me.

The speed at which I made the first team was also a startling experience for me. Earlier that season, when I'd come back from France, I had played a couple of games for Hinckley Colts and then gone over to Leicester to join the Tigers in mid-February. And now, only about eight weeks later, here I was making my debut for the first XV.

After the win at Neath, there was one more game on our Easter tour in South Wales. This was at Pontypool, which at that time was probably about as warm and friendly a place to go as Siberia on a January night. Fortunately, I was dropped for the game. They gave us a bit of a hiding that day but the lad who filled in for me, Duncan Black, played outstandingly well. He seemed to spend the entire game getting up from close-contact situations like tackles, rucks and mauls and promptly being flattened again. On one occasion, he was having treatment for a heavy knock and I got off the bench and started to warm up with some stretching exercises. The legendary Ray Prosser, coach of Pontypool at that time and renowned as a hard man throughout Wales, looked across at me and said: 'I don't know what you're warming up for, boy – you won't be on that pitch too long even if you get out there!'

I was temporarily lost for words, but after a moment I shot back: 'Actually, I'm sharpening up my studs for the game.' Even today, years later, I can still see the look on his face at that retort. I wasted no time in jogging back to the bench and quickly sitting down, hoping and praying that no one would come off! That Pontypool game was another stage on the learning curve – it was far harder than the Neath match had been.

Mixing with first-team players at a senior club like Leicester and finding myself at the Neaths and Pontypools of this world was a far cry from my life of only a few months earlier. When I came home from France, a friend of the family, a chap called Bill Brown, who has sadly recently died, suggested I went along to Leicester. Bill had links with Coventry and Leicester from his playing days and said he thought I'd like Welford Road best. He had a word with some of his old friends who were on the committee by then, and I was invited to go over for training.

Before going to France I'd had a very loose connection with Hinckley, the junior club nearest to my home. I used to turn out for my school, John Cleveland College, in the town on Saturday mornings and then get showered and changed and rush over to Hinckley's ground to play in a fourth- or fifth-team game in the afternoon. All my schoolfriends went to Hinckley to play their rugby but I never stayed long enough to make the first team there.

I think my life began to change from that first night when my father drove me over to Leicester for my first-ever training session with the club. I remember it vividly. It was a very wet March night in 1982, and as I had not yet passed my driving test, Dad took me and waited in the car while I trained. I was put in with the youth team, of course, but it fairly quickly became obvious, to both me and the coach, that I ought to be able to cope with a higher standard. I had, after all, played in French club rugby for some months, and, while I don't want to sound condescending, the transition from French first-team rugby to the Leicester youth team hardly stretched me. English youth rugby was never going to be as tough or physical as what goes on over in France.

So after two training sessions, it was suggested that I joined the senior squad for training. It was there that I encountered Chalkie White for the first time. Chalkie, who, by the time he retired, came to be respected the length and breadth of the land, had begun to make a name for himself. He was a coach who did not always do the expected thing, nor did he necessarily discuss the obvious points. He looked at the game from an angle you wouldn't have thought of, but when you followed his line of thinking, you realized that he was right. He thought very, very deeply about rugby and his players' roles in it.

When I first went to Leicester as an 18-year-old, I had a preconceived idea as to what sort of a club it was. I suppose in my naivety I thought it was going to be run along the lines of Leicester City Football Club, or even Manchester United. Leicester Tigers have always enjoyed a fine reputation and their image is – and rightly so – one of a major club, but at that age I had no idea just what that meant. The club had recently enjoyed significant success in the English Cup finals. The major organized Cup competition in England had only got off the ground in 1972, but it was not until 1978 that Leicester reached their first final, which they lost 6–3 to Gloucester. However, that appearance was the turning point for the club. They contested the next three Cup finals and won every one to claim for ever the original John Player Cup. In 1979 they beat Moseley 15–12; in 1980 London Irish succumbed by 21–9 and in 1981 they claimed the scalp of Gosforth – who had already won the Cup twice before (in 1976 and 1977) – by 22–15. Little wonder, then, that when I joined the Tigers I looked upon them as the premier rugby club in the country. Furthermore, England had won a Grand Slam in 1980 with a team which contained four players from Leicester – Dusty Hare, Paul Dodge, Clive Woodward and Peter Wheeler.

This solid wedge of internationals was mixed with many other fine players: people like Gary Adey, Les Cusworth and Robin Cowling – all of whom had already been capped by England (Cusworth, in fact, was later to be recalled to the national side). There were the loyal club servants, too: Steve Johnson, Terry Burwell, Tim Barnwell, Stuart Redfern, Nick Joyce, Nick Gillingham, Ian Smith and Steve Kenney were all highly proficient players able to produce and sustain a high quality of play.

Given all this, what I discovered at Welford Road when I first arrived came as something of a shock. I found a club basically run by an army of volunteers. It was very old-fashioned and, until quite recently, the system remained much the same. From the club secretary to the treasurer, from the president to the match secretary and coaches, the whole thing was organized and planned by people who gave their time for free, juggling their commitments with the demands of important day jobs and families. It was quite extraordinary. And yet the organization at Leicester, from well before that time right through to today, some thirteen years later, has always been second to none. These people, who do it only for the love of the game and the club in particular, put so much into ensuring that the club is run smoothly and efficiently. Nowadays, when everyone seems preoccupied with getting something out of every situation, it is wonderfully refreshing to see Leicester still maintained by and large by that army of willing volunteers. Today, though, there are a few people at Leicester Rugby Club who do receive a salary – people such as the director of rugby, Tony Russ, who does a magnificent job. His is a full-time post which makes a major contribution not only to the present-day success of the club but to building for a future just as bright. The secretaries and administrator/director also receive proper wages. Years ago, only the groundsman was paid.

It is my belief that things are bound to change still further over the coming years, for I cannot see how a serious First Division club in England can for ever be run on the basis of good people giving their time for nothing. The increasing influence of money within the game, which I regard as inevitable, will, I think, help to bring about this sea change. I can foresee a situation in which amateur volunteers will begin to question why they are receiving nothing for their efforts while an increasing number of paid officers at a rugby club receive handsome salaries. I am not saying there will be open animosity, but I do anticipate a certain amount of reluctance on the part of many people to do something for nothing.

This will be a very difficult area for the game in the future. No one can deny that, to take the case of one of our salaried staff, Tony Russ has proved himself worth his weight in gold. Besides, the position Tony took over was one that only a full-time person could fulfil. Had the work he does been left to a couple of loyal club servants to fit in during some hours in the evenings, I don't believe Leicester would have got as far as they have today. It was essential that a paid person was taken on, and I suspect that this will increasingly be the case for many other positions at the club.

As time goes by and the game becomes still more commercial in its outlook, you are going to have to have somebody in a professional, full-time capacity running a major club. I see the secretary's role becoming more like that of a chief executive, and clubs like Leicester are going to have to be prepared to find a salary commensurate with that job and the experience required to do it. And if a paid official does take on that job full time, maybe clubs will become still more efficient. It goes without saying that they would have to be pretty careful in deciding how to spend their money and whom they recruit, but that should not be too much of a problem for senior clubs like Leicester, Bath and Harlequins.

At the beginning, of course, I was more preoccupied with attempting to win a first-team place on something like a regular basis than with questions like this. Gary Adey had retired and the Tigers were looking for a new No. 8. They had a chap at the club called Angus Collington, whom I thought looked a pretty useful player. But for some reason they didn't think he was the one for the future, perhaps because he wasn't quite tall enough. So the following season, 1982–3, I played my second first-team game, a 21–8 win over Richmond on 9 October.

Even in those early days, the conflict between my job and my sport was making itself felt. I was due to play my third match for the seniors against Cambridge University, which included in that year, for the first time, a certain C. R. Andrew. But because of police duties at Filbert Street for Leicester City's home soccer match against Newcastle, I had to miss the rugby game. I have long since lost count of the number of times the two have clashed. Often, I have been unable to play because I've been working, or I have had to dash from work, where I might have finished a Saturday morning shift at 2 p.m., to get to Welford Road in time for the 3 p.m. kick-off. I want to say here and now that I am eternally grateful to my colleagues and seniors in the force who have helped to enable me to play as much rugby as I have done over the past thirteen years. It has not always been easy, for them or for me.

The 1982–3 season, which I had begun in the hope of securing a first-team place, ended astonishingly with one D. Richards running out for the Tigers in the John Player Cup final at Twickenham. To reach the final we beat High Wycombe, Wakefield, Harlequins and London Scottish, but at Twickenham, although the match itself was described as the best Cup final there had ever been, there was little for Leicester or me to celebrate. Bristol beat us 28–22, even though we had been favourites to win our fourth Cup in five years.

It was an emotional day for us at the end of an emotional season, during which Chalkie White had bid us farewell, a moving experience, especially for the older hands at the club. And Steve Johnson, our captain, made the final his last game before retirement. There was for me a hard lesson to be learned from that day. I tried to pick up the ball on our own line when we were under heavy pressure. We'd had a scrum about five yards from our own line and the scrum wheeled. Instead of consolidating, I picked it up and started to drive forward, but somehow I lost the ball. Bristol went right and Bob Hesford scored in the corner. It is something you should not do – pick up on your own line, become isolated and lose possession. I should have allowed the scrum-half to clear. I knew at once I'd made a major mistake and when Bristol scored from it, I felt awful. The fact that a record crowd for those days of thirty-three thousand was there to see it made it even worse. I had been very nervous before that game. I had played before at Twickenham, when we met Harlequins in an early-season club fixture, but not in the highly charged atmosphere of a Cup final. It wasn't so much the sight of the famous old ground as the noise that those thirty-three thousand supporters made all the afternoon. I found that quite nerve-racking.

Chalkie slipped into the dressing room afterwards and had a word with me. So did Ian Smith. I went through the incident and knew what I'd done. In the final reckoning, I don't think it was that error which cost us the game, but nevertheless it was a clear mistake from which Bristol had scored a try, and I was bitterly disappointed. I'd come a long way in twelve or eighteen months: from making my debut at Leicester to playing in an English Cup final. It was quite a turnaround. And, as I said earlier, already the demands of my new job in the police force were making life quite difficult for me in terms of my sport. In fact, the night before that final, I'd had to work until 2 a.m. and didn't get to bed until almost 3. I was up at 8.30 to drive down to Twickenham on the morning of the game. I felt shattered.

A second incident in that game was another bad blow for Leicester. Tim Barnwell suffered a very serious injury which was to end his career. He got a heavy knock, and at first we thought he was just concussed, but we realized after the match that he was in a pretty bad way. Everybody was very concerned for him. He was rushed to hospital with a blood clot on the brain and needed an immediate operation. Happily, he came through it and is now fine. He comes down to the club quite often and reports on the radio for the BBC in Leicester with Bleddyn Jones.

We played that final without our kicking machine Dusty Hare, who had been selected for the 1983 British Lions tour of New Zealand and did not want to jeopardize his tour by risking injury in the Cup final. We understood his decision, and in any case, it wasn't because Dusty was missing that we failed to win.

The key factor was that we gave Bristol some easy tries, and we had only ourselves to blame for the defeat. Had we played a tighter game I think we would have won. But is it reasonable to play a tight game with a back line that includes Cusworth, Dodge, Woodward and Youngs? Besides, the free-flowing way we played that day was the way Leicester played rugby, and always have done. I would never criticize the Leicester style. At times it is breathtaking – literally.

In all, I played twenty-six times for the Tigers in that first full season of 1982–3. And I scored six tries. That was a reflection of the desire of the side to score tries, no matter who ended up dotting the ball down over our opponents' goal-line. Leicester have always played the type of rugby which attempts to bring everybody into the game. We were certainly spinning the ball around in those days, making full use of the likes of Woodward, Dodge, Cusworth, Evans, Barnwell and Williams, not to mention Hare, who would come into the back line as another attacker. It worked and it was a lot of fun.

People remarked on the progress I had made and some started to tip me for future international honours. But to be honest, I had not even thought about that. I wasn't aware that I was improving that much; I was just enjoying myself, playing good rugby. I didn't find it too difficult and I seemed to be able to keep up with the play quite easily. It was a pleasure to play alongside the players Leicester had then, and in those days rugby was still a game played essentially for the pleasure of it. Of course, you wanted to win cups, but the mentality was quite different from the serious regimes of today. For example, people saw nothing wrong in going out after a training session in the week and having four or five pints of beer. They'd have a few the night before a game, too – even on the eve of an international. I never used to do it myself, but often I'd see players who had been out and supped three, four or five pints the night before a match. It didn't seem to affect them.

To my mind, those were the best days. You played your rugby hard and seriously, and high standards were demanded, but at the end of the day you tended to judge what you had experienced on whether it had been fun. That yardstick no longer applies, and I have to say that I think rugby has lost something now that fun element has all but vanished. The will to win has increased threefold; the costs are high and the price of defeat in any match can be enormous. If you lose a League game or two it could mean the difference between winning the title or being relegated, depending on your position in the table, and no side can any longer afford to lose at the expense of everyone playing a jolly good game of attacking, entertaining rugby. There is now at almost all levels of the game a win-at-all-costs attitude, and I am not sure rugby is the better for that. It is better, perhaps, in the sense that standards are higher and there has been a significant knock-on effect for the England international side – an improvement I will come to later – but not in terms of the spirit and enjoyment to be extracted from ordinary club matches on a Saturday afternoon. Too many of these have become boring, predictable slogs for the two League points on offer. That is a pity, in my view.

I suppose the type of characters we remember from the early 1980s do still exist in the modern game, but perhaps they are now to be found at a different level of the sport. At the top clubs, I cannot believe you would find many players these days popping into their local pub for a few pints after training on a Wednesday or Thursday night. You just wouldn't do it. Many players will not even drink on the Saturday night after a game in case it interferes with their carefully worked-out fitness training programme. Those programmes undoubtedly lead players to superior fitness, but whether they give them as much old-fashioned fun is another matter entirely.

I was fortunate to come into the Leicester side at a time when they had some very strong characters from whom you could learn. The first person I really looked up to was Steve Johnson, also a policeman. He was captain in my first year at Leicester and was one of those guys who would always lead from the front. He was unlucky not to get a cap. To suggest that I

modelled myself on him would be wide of the mark, though –
you don't model yourself on anybody. I have never done that,
and I hope that nobody else ever regards me as his role model.
You should have your own style and stick to it, because each
person has his own attributes. Johnno, who gained the utmost
respect from everyone because he led so forcefully, is now doing
very well as a police superintendent in Leicestershire.

Peter Wheeler was also around, and I'd heard so much about
him that I regarded it as an honour to play alongside him in
my first season. Unfortunately, he didn't hang around for too
many seasons afterwards. It is difficult to describe Peter. He is
very quiet in his own way – charming, too – but he had a killer
instinct, a fierce will to win. He was an outstanding footballer
who clearly should have won another Lions tour place in 1983.

Other familiar faces tended to come and go, as they do at
every club, but what struck me most about the Tigers was their
basic stability. To me, the secret of Leicester's success is that
almost all the committees and the coaching staff are made up
of ex-players. The club has always tried to follow through and
pick the right staff to continue to contribute when their playing
careers are over. This means that those charged with the important decision-making, whether it affects the club off the field or
the players actually on it, know what is required at Leicester.
They understand the Leicester way. This continuity has also
tended to keep out the type who wants to come in on the back
of our success, perhaps just to make a name or a quick buck
for himself. We don't have those people at the club – all those
involved at Welford Road are in it for the good of the club
itself, not themselves. They have decided that they want to put
something back into the club by working behind the scenes.

Many of the retired players on the coaching side are Leicester
men through and through: Dosser Smith, Paul Dodge, Kevin
McDonald and Stuart Redfern, to name just a few. I imagine
plenty of others will follow a similar path in the future: already
people like Andy Key and Steve Kenney are coming through.
In a few years' time, when they become too old to coach, they

will probably go on to committees at the club and some of the players from the current era will take up the coaching duties. It is like a succession, really, a guaranteed production line of personnel who have a certain feeling for the Tigers. And the only way they have attained that affinity is by having played for Leicester at some stage. Of course, there are people on committees at the club who have not played for us, but they too are Leicester people and they understand what the Tigers mean to the city and the area.

They work so hard, I am sure, because Leicester has a certain charisma, something that perhaps no other club in England possesses. You either like it or you don't, but I have never really met anyone who has been to Leicester and doesn't like the club. There is a genuine warmth to the welcome offered to outsiders when they visit Welford Road. Many visiting teams and their officials remark upon it, and as Leicester men we are justifiably proud of that.

However, to be completely honest, from my own experiences it has perhaps not always been that way. When I first joined Leicester, it was very insular and I found life very difficult for the first couple of seasons. I felt I was not accepted, and I put that down to the fact that a lot of the players – people such as Stuart and Steve Redfern and Wayne Richardson – had come through the ranks of youth rugby for Leicester. At the time there was a very strong youth policy and they had served their apprenticeship, if you like, in the lower levels of the club and were accepted as true Leicester men.

My background, on the other hand, was quite different. I had come out of nowhere virtually straight into the first team, and I think that came as a bit of a shock to some people at the club. I could not say I was exactly shunned, but undeniably it was not as easy for my team-mates to get on with an outsider like myself as with the boys who had come up through the ranks. I had the unmistakable feeling that they resented a youngster of whom they had never heard coming in and taking over one of their friends' slots in the team. Perhaps the best way of putting it is that I wasn't one of the family. I am now, of course. It was by no means impossible to integrate and settle, but I think you were certainly expected to give rather more than you took.

I found this process of initiation, for want of a better word, coming chiefly from the playing side. The officials at Leicester are by and large very good and have no compunction about somebody being brought in and, if he is good enough, being played in the senior side. On the contrary, they welcome you with open arms, as I'm sure a great many other incoming players have discovered.

I should say that this slight undercurrent did not cause me any undue problems, but all the same it was undoubtedly there. Thankfully, the feeling of not belonging didn't last too long. Since then, a couple of other 'outsiders' have asked me whether I ever noticed it, which rather confirmed my initial suspicions. I had the impression that I needed to win the respect of the players through what I did on the field to be fully accepted, and of course in time that gradually happened.

Leicester is still very much a family club, although, having said that, over the last five or six years a lot more 'outsiders' have joined us. It is my firm belief that their presence has made us a better club, for it is more open and outgoing now, and all the stronger for that.

3 Tigers Triumph

After our near miss in the Cup final of 1983 against Bristol, our glorious run of success in the tournament came to a complete halt for a few seasons. Coventry, our midlands rivals who have fallen upon such hard times of late, put us out at the third-round stage in 1984, winning a tough derby match 13–9. And just twelve months later, it was Coventry again who ended our hopes, this time in the quarter-final, going through to the semis on the greater-number-of-tries-scored rule after a 10–10 draw. Coventry's joy that year was short-lived – they also drew 10–10 in their semi-final against London Welsh and missed out on a place in the final because the Welsh had scored more tries. We knew how they felt! The 1986 John Player Cup was to prove another letdown for us. We went down 6–10 to Bath on our own ground, Simon Halliday crossing for the only try of a tight semi-final.

Individual matches and famous tries come and go. They are exciting at the time, of course, and provide a warm glow of pleasure and satisfaction. But I don't want to reflect on my long association with Leicester simply by recounting a long list of individual matches, famous wins and disappointing defeats. For me, there is so much more to a great rugby club than results. Sure, they bear an increasing importance in the modern-day game, but they can never be the whole story of a club. I believe that the heart and soul, the real memory of a rugby club, is its people, its loyal servants who have laboured long weeks, months and years in the cause of the club, and its regular supporters, who travel near and far to support their team. Rugby Union is fortunate in that so many people seem ready and willing to contribute just about wherever the game is played around the world. That, perhaps, is the true strength of our game: the willingness of others to give generously, whether it be in terms of time or finance, to assist their clubs.

Leicester has had some splendid servants over the years, none probably better than John Allen, known affectionately as Gubby to one and all (but beware – it is not a nickname he likes!). John has been a mainstay of the club and his contribution is second to none. What he achieves in an administrative capacity is simply outstanding. He is rightly regarded as the rock on which the club has stood. He played for Leicester for many years and was a very good scrum-half. Like so many others, after his playing career finished, he served in other ways. He is down at the club first thing in the morning, you will see him there at lunchtime and he'll pop back in the evening to tidy up some more work on club matters. He is a partner in an accountancy firm in Leicester and I cannot believe he does not find it hard to devote so much time and fit in so many commitments for the rugby club. Stories about Gubby are renowned throughout the game in this part of the world. Try pulling a fast one on him and you have about as much chance as there is of a players' wild night out on the eve of an international not appearing in the tabloids. Gubby is red hot on the question of expenses. I've even known him pore over a player's mileage claim, suspecting it to be, shall we say, incorrectly gauged, and get into his car to go and measure the precise distance himself. And then he'll tell the player what he's done and why he has cut back his expenses. John has always kept a very shrewd eye on expenses claims, and to be fair to him, certain people have tried to abuse the system in the past.

David Matthews is also a Tigers man through and through. He still holds the record for the most first-team appearances for the Tigers, 502, and he has not lost the ability to read a game and to look at it from a completely different perspective from anybody else. David was involved on the coaching side in the late 1980s and he remains a selector. He played openside flanker, so he tends to watch the back-row area of the game with as keen an eye as anyone. Sometimes he will pass on some thoughts from a match and I am always prepared to listen to anything that comes from him. He will often pick up on something you have not thought about. I very much respect his judgement.

There are so many people I could mention that inevitably, by naming some and not others, I may hurt equally worthy souls. If your name has not appeared then I can but plead an aberration brought on by temporary memory loss. One player I could not possibly forget is John Wells. He was captain for two years, taking over from me after my first two-year stint. When John completed his term, I took on the reins again. I feel proud to have been asked on two separate occasions to become captain of Leicester, and I know that John felt a similar pride in the job. He joined the Tigers the season after me and we have become very close, literally so in the case of on-the-field activities, and off the pitch, too. He is the type of player who has always been under-estimated. He has never been one of these big hitters who has stood out and done all the running off. Instead he does the hard work required of a back-row forward. He is one of the real players who has made our side tick – and you cannot say that of everyone. He has the grit, determination and will to win which some lack. I think in the mid-1980s, when England were struggling for a blindside flanker before Mike Teague rejoined the side, John Wells should have been given a chance.

I should also like to mention the contribution of Tudor Thomas, who, besides doing so much for the club, was also an usher at my wedding. We let him do that even though he is Welsh, which surely shows commendable generosity on the part of an Englishman. In my early years at Welford Road, it was chiefly Tudor who took my wife, Nicky, and myself under his wing and looked after us. He was always extremely hospitable to us both. At the club he took on loads of duties, from being match secretary to ensuring that all the kit was cleaned, ironed and ready for the next game. And he was the Marje Proops of the club: if anybody had any problems they went to Tudor, and he invariably helped them out. He was always there to talk to. He stepped down from that role about two years ago and has been club president more recently.

Chalkie White I shall always remember with the utmost respect and admiration. In truth, he was only there for a short period – about a year – when I was around, but in that time he helped me launch my career on the right lines. Chalkie was a thinking man's coach, one of those people who had the universal respect of all the players, the committee men and the opposition as well. Like David Matthews, he would pick out points in a game and bring them up for discussion later, making you think about them and analyse them, perhaps in a different light. Chalkie was perhaps the most admired coach we have ever had at Leicester, and of course he earned his accolades through his conspicuous success. But having said that, I feel that the current combination of Ian Smith and Paul Dodge is proving highly effective, and they could develop into an extremely successful duo themselves. The number of games we lose seems to be dropping each year.

Leicester have undoubtedly benefited from having so many recently retired players available for coaching roles. Not necessarily all the best coaches are former players, but I do think that players who have been involved comparatively recently can contribute modern ideas which are hugely to the advantage of any team. I find it difficult to believe that people who have been retired for a number of years can suddenly come back to it and fully understand how the modern game is developing and how it has evolved in the time they have been away. Over the last ten or fifteen years, for example, rugby has become so much faster and it is now played by people who are much fitter. Today, people think about the game in more depth and with greater analysis. Players twenty years ago just didn't do those things.

I am delighted that Leicester is not a club which puts its players through hours and hours of video film for the purpose of studying every movement, whim and trick of the opposition. While I acknowledge that watching videos is much more important than ever before if you want to have a proper idea of what your opponents are likely to get up to, I have to say I find the whole thing thoroughly boring. Tony Russ tends to look at the videos on our behalf and then give us a full appraisal of the opposition. So if any Tigers fans feel that we have lost a match because we have not been fully prepared for something the opposition has done, don't blame the players. I recommend forwarding all complaints to Tony.

Seriously, though, the nature of the modern game demands that someone has to do all this preparation if you want to know about the strengths and weaknesses of your opponents. Imagine trying to find someone to take on all this if Tony were not a paid employee of the club.

Over the years, you become familiar with certain clubs and relish the prospect of meeting them. Others you somehow never look forward to playing. I always used to dread going to the Welsh clubs such as Swansea, Pontypool and Neath. Leicester had a reputation in those days for playing very attractive rugby, but we rarely had a front five to match the intensity and sheer physicality of the Welsh packs. Our players were often easy meat for the Welsh boys, so consequently none of our lads ever enjoyed going there. Apart from anything else, there was nothing really at stake so there wasn't a lot of point in going down there to get a good sorting out – or at least, that seemed to be the reasoning in those days!

But the story of Leicester Rugby Club in recent years has been one of extraordinary success. Look at the Tigers who contributed so much to England's 1980 Grand Slam success. Look at those who participated in the back-to-back Grand Slams England achieved in 1991 and 1992. Then there is the Cup: winners in 1979, 1980 and 1981; winners again in 1993 and beaten finalists in 1978, 1983, 1989 and 1994. And, of course, the League victory in 1995. Some record – and a tribute to the consistently high standards achieved by a succession of officials, coaches and players at Welford Road.

There have been wonderful achievements and deeply disappointing defeats. Getting to a Cup final is terrific, but if you lose it, the sense of dismay comes crowding in when you reflect on the fact that you have come so near, yet ended up so far, from real glory.

I am sometimes asked how I see the future for a club like Leicester. My answer is that it depends very much on whether rugby as a whole and the club itself remain amateur. If the game does go professional and we decide to remain strictly amateur, then we would fall behind – I don't think there is any doubt about that. So it is imperative that we watch carefully to see what lead is provided by the RFU, and stick with it. But the way forward for the Tigers will probably depend on who we have on the committee at that time. I personally hope that Leicester will hold true to its principles. We are a club without hypocrisy; we do not say one thing publicly and then do the complete opposite behind closed doors. We are not like that, but I have to say that not every club is run the same way.

There have been times when our honesty and willingness to follow the rules and not make a nonsense of the amateur regulations have cost us the services of some fine players. There are players who have not joined Leicester because the material rewards have not been there. It would serve no purpose to name them; what happened was a private business between them and our club. But we know that certain high-quality players who would have been major acquisitions for us did not come to us in the end because there was nothing in it for them. That was their choice. Those people were treated no differently from anybody else when we heard that they might like to join us. They were firmly told that we do not provide a free car, there are no generous 'expenses' and the home dressing room at Welford Road has never seen any little brown envelopes after matches. Each player, if he comes to us, gets what everybody else gets, and that is 20p a mile travelling allowance for training and playing. No more.

I would be the first to say that I fully support the club in its view that we should not bend the rules. I don't want to see a superstar join Leicester chiefly because we have been influenced by his name and reputation to the extent that we've said, 'Let's give him what he wants.' The Tigers have proved conclusively that no player is bigger than the club itself, and I believe that is cause for considerable pride. Players who come to Leicester must want to come, partly because of the spirit and tradition, but also because we play the right type of rugby and you can get on to the ladder as a player there. If what I hear is the truth, too many ordinary players around England are receiving material rewards which are not permitted in the laws and of which they are not worthy.

I think that if we did pay top players, the team spirit at the club would be damaged. We know at the moment that no single person is receiving a benefit denied to others. That breeds good team morale and a common purpose. We have recently set up a players' trust fund, and we should find out within the next year whether this is causing any problems. I can't see any major difficulties because it will be managed by the players, so there shouldn't be any disputes about who gets what. Everything will be fairly divided.

Leicester keep a tight watch on money-related matters because they believe in the principle of an amateur game. Nevertheless, they go out of their way to provide the best facilities they can manage for the players. We are very well looked after. There is a handsomely equipped gym; physiotherapy is provided free, and there is as much of it as you need or want. So the back-up facilities are excellent, and when you run out on to the pitch, you step on to the best playing surface in the country. But of course, all that will never be enough for those players who want money and cars.

Some players become unhappy after a time. If they don't get a certain number of first-team games they want to leave; they think they deserve better. But the club won't be held to ransom, and again, I support that stance. My view is that if you are good enough, you will get in. It is perhaps the players who are not quite of the highest calibre, and who therefore struggle to make it, who end up dissatisfied and drift away elsewhere. The trouble is, some people don't realize that you have to wait a certain amount of time before a position becomes available. They are not willing to be patient; they want a first-team place immediately. The presence of that sort of person in our club concerns me, because it puts us in an awkward situation. There are undeniably some guys we would like to keep at the club, and we feel that in the long run it would be better for them if they did stay. But often a player in this situation does not look far enough into the future. He lacks the vision of his more experienced colleagues and especially of the committee at Leicester. Some of them may scoff at what they see as old-fashioned rules, but you only have to look at the facts to see that this club has got an awful lot going for it.

We have ten thousand members with a ceiling imposed at that level, and there are said to be another few thousand on the waiting list for membership. We hope to satisfy that demand by the reconstruction and enlargement of the ground over the next few years. There will be a new stand, an extended clubhouse and a greater capacity. The maximum gate we can fit in now is around sixteen thousand, but when the work is completed that will rise to about twenty-two thousand. In all it will cost around five million pounds, and you cannot contemplate development on that scale unless you have some pretty shrewd people with their heads screwed on the right way working behind the scenes. Otherwise, you run the risk of suffering the fate of the old Rugby RFC, which collapsed financially after building a big new clubhouse.

Rugby Union today is something of a paradox, because on one hand you have these amateur rules, and on the other a need for a strong financial base and considerable experience to run

modern clubs as businesses. While that may seem a contradic-
tion in terms, I think we just have to get on with it as long as
the laws stay as they are. And there are not too many clubs
able to develop to this extent, nor many which can boast such
a large membership with people queuing up to join. A major
reason for all this support and interest is that Leicester is a
charming club. I just hope it retains that charm, together with
its exemplary attitude, because if it ever lost it I am sure it
would simply not be the same. I have a personal pride and
affection for the club and I wouldn't like to see the standards
drop. I cannot see any real reason why they should — unless
every other club became professional, in the true meaning of
the word, and we were left behind because we retained our
principles. I hope I am never around to see that happen.

I have heard many people say it and I share the view: Leicester
is different. Some of its characters have probably helped make
it so. Someone like Graham Willars, for instance.

Graham has a lifelong association with the club. He first
played for the Tigers in the 1959–60 season and has been coach
and more recently club president. One image of him will always
stick in my mind. In 1984, when Graham was coach, we went
to Swansea for a game, which we lost 25–12. When we left the
ground for the Dragon Hotel in the centre of Swansea, where
we were staying, we couldn't find Graham. It turned out he'd
hitched a lift back to the hotel. Later, we headed off to a local
pub called the Cricketers and were just crossing the road when
we heard the sound of a car screeching around corners. When
it came into sight, its lights were blazing and it was twisting
and turning and going all over the place. Suddenly, we spotted
a figure on the roof, desperately trying to hang on for dear life.
Not surprisingly, we were all thoroughly alarmed. When the
car pulled up beside the pub, who should clamber down off the
roof, dust himself down and announce himself ready for a pint
but Graham Willars. We couldn't believe our eyes. Apparently,
this guy had told him that his car was full but he was more
than willing to take him on the roof. Graham was happy enough

with this arrangement – until he discovered that the driver's idea of a joke was to try to unseat his extra passenger!

Another terrific character at the club was Harry Roberts. Harry was a real man's man. Nobody could have accused him of being one of the club's prima donnas. He had once been blown up in an ambush while on patrol for the Rhodesian army. He had seen a lot of his best friends blown to pieces in that incident and he'd also suffered phosphorus burns across much of his body, not to mention losing a few teeth. Anyway, Harry's party trick was to repair his own broken body. Unfortunately, although he was a hooker, he had two poor shoulders and often they would dislocate. He used to ask the referee to hang on a minute, twist his body around, somehow manipulate his arm as his face contorted in pain and put the joint back in. Then he'd pack down for the next scrum. He was a tremendous trainer, which was fortunate, because he was equally as good at drinking, which he enjoyed greatly. In other words, he lived life to the full.

In my time at the club, I have played in sides captained by Steve Johnson, Ian Smith, Les Cusworth, Paul Dodge and John Wells. All had different styles of captaincy. Johnson was tough, very abrupt and what he said went. Dosser Smith gives his life and soul to the club. I have a lot of time for him because he is what Leicester is all about. Les was different again, a good tactician. I felt that John Wells, who followed me, captained very capably. He was a very, very good skipper who led from the front, and the majority of the decisions he made were the right ones. Of course, they all had individual attributes, but if pushed I think I'd have to say that for me John Wells was perhaps the best captain of all.

All these players sometimes had to face an unreasonable level of violence. Tim Barnwell came off in one Welsh match with a badly cut eye after being kicked in the head. I have no doubt that it was done deliberately. It is strange that, having occupied such a position of eminence that even the top English clubs felt uncomfortable about going down to Wales because they feared the confrontation and likely defeat, Welsh club rugby has stagnated. I'm not sure it has actually gone backwards, but I think it has hit a plateau, certainly compared with the enormously improved standards in England. I anticipate that it will be at least another couple of years before the Welsh can go forward from this situation.

Take a look at English club rugby today. There are no longer any easy games. Go back just ten years to 1984–5, and compare Leicester's fixture list and some of the results. In that season, we played clubs as far apart (geographically as well as in terms of standards) as Richmond, Nuneaton, Bath, Birmingham, Neath, Pontypool, Cambridge University, Nottingham, Blackheath, London Welsh, the RAF and the Royal Navy. We had victories by margins such as 41–4, 55–21, 33–9, 50–14, 42–3, 40–16 and 38–6. But we also lost matches to Bath, Swansea, Cardiff, Pontypool, Bristol and Gloucester, among others. Such an alarming variation in the quality of the opposition did not do us much good. Winning 55–21 one week and then losing the next is not the way to achieve consistency. This situation no longer exists in English club rugby – not in the First Division of the Courage Leagues, anyway – and as a result, the consistency of a side like Leicester has vastly improved. We might lose to Bath, and perhaps somewhere that is always tricky, such as Bristol or Gloucester. But the reality is that we lose very few games indeed, and nowadays you do not see the wild fluctuations in our form which occurred ten years ago.

In Wales, meanwhile, the top sides are still winning some matches, even in the Heineken Leagues, by sixty or seventy points. That cannot be healthy. To thrive at international level you have got to be able to handle the pressure. How better to do that than by playing hard Courage League matches each week? I believe that the Welsh should cut down the size of their Leagues and play fewer games, but against better sides. That would make each game a lot more intense and much harder. Then everything would be geared towards a higher level. Of course, the idea of a European League has been suggested, and there is no doubt that it would greatly benefit the players of Wales, Scotland and Ireland, whose club systems at present do not begin to compare with the English formula. Apart from for financial reasons (which will probably decide matters in the coming years) I don't think that English club rugby has any need for a European League. When you have clubs like Northampton and Harlequins, two clubs which can boast several familiar international players, propping up the bottom of the English First Division – and in the case of Northampton in 1995, subsequently even sinking into Division 2 – then that tells you something about the strength of the English club structure.

Of the many other clubs Leicester have always played, one of those I have most enjoyed facing is Bath. It is always a very hard physical contest, and it is usually clean. They may have frustrated us many times in recent seasons as we sought League titles and Pilkington Cups and they used to have a reputation as being a dirty side, although I have never really come across that save for on one occasion. The incident that marred my appreciation of the club was when one of their international players kicked John Wells in the mouth. It was a nasty injury – he needed twelve stitches in the wound – and it seemed to have been inflicted intentionally. The player in question will know who I am talking about, and both John Wells and I know. There is no need for that sort of incident. I have never been one for kicking people in the head and I find it extremely disturbing that a minority of players would do that. I have to say that I have never had the slightest time for him ever since that day.

Happily, I think the number of players who set out to kick someone deliberately is declining nowadays. With the advent of cameras and videos you are too easily caught, and bearing in mind that people can now take you to court, rugby players generally do not risk it.

I greatly prefer playing at Bath to Gloucester. For me, the noisy and abusive Kingsholm crowd spoil it for them. The first time I ever went to Gloucester to play, as usual half the Leicester side was missing. It was a cold Wednesday night at the start of

December – conditions not to the liking of the Leicester boys at all. Nevertheless, we won the match 21–10, to which Dusty Hare contributed a try, two conversions and three penalty goals. It wasn't very often teams went down there and won, especially not Leicester. And although more recently we have won there a few more times, it is not one of the most pleasurable places I have played. In 1995, our defeat in the League match in Gloucester after Christmas was a serious setback in our chase for the Courage League Championship title.

I'm not keen on the crowds or atmosphere at Bristol, either. Bath is somewhat different, and I have got on better with the Bath boys over the years. Of course, I have had the chance to get to know players like Nigel Redman, Graham Dawe, Andy Robinson and Jerry Guscott with the England squad. There are always exceptions, though, and Mike Teague was a close friend and a good after-match companion whenever we went to Gloucester. I spent one memorable night with him after our team coach broke down practically before it was out of the Kingsholm car park. The driver estimated it would take two or three hours to fix and Teaguey and I made sure that that time was utilized to the full. He took me off into the town around some splendid local inns. By the time we got back to the ground for me to join up with the others for the journey home, I was happily drunk.

You struggle to find any sort of atmosphere at the grounds of the two major London clubs, Harlequins and Wasps. What a contrast there is between those two and the big clubs of the south-west. Even if you don't particularly like the crowds at Gloucester or Bristol, you cannot deny that they are vociferous and passionate. At Wasps and Quins it is difficult to detect any atmosphere at all. The Stoop, the Quins ground, is awful and at Wasps it is little better. I put it down to regional differences – rugby is more of a middle-class, stiff-upper-lip sport in the south-east. Those London clubs also lack the strong identity of representing a whole town in the way that Leicester and Bath do. Another ground I confess I don't like visiting is

Northampton. For years, they had a group of supporters who made a shocking noise which must have been more of an irritation to the home team than an encouragement. The other midlands clubs are not much better: Moseley is like a ghost club these days and I've never looked forward to playing at Coventry. Moseley still seem to think they should be the number one club in the midlands, but they have lost their way as to how to go about achieving that.

Of the midlands clubs, I think Coventry could get back to their old position of strength. The trouble is that there is a general lack of ability on the coaching front in midlands rugby at the moment. As I have explained, Leicester have developed their own former players to fill the coaching roles and generally they have done quite well. But other clubs in the region seem to want to import coaches. They have come from far and wide, and almost every one has been a failure. In truth, the clubs who have recruited these people have not had their house in order first. This approach worked for only one club during one period, and that was at Northampton in the Wayne Shelford years. It succeeded because of Shelford's exceptional ability and knowledge, but there are not too many people like him in the world. I think that Coventry, Moseley and Nottingham will continue to struggle until they actually get the structure of their clubs right. I hope it does not sound pompous to say so, but that is one thing which Leicester have always had sorted out.

It is a shame that other clubs in the midlands have declined so dramatically because there used to be some great local derbies. In recent years no club has been able to match Leicester – apart from Northampton, who succeeded briefly in the higher regions of the First Division before being relegated in May 1995. Their problem is that they have had four years of being there or thereabouts but have come away with nothing. Had they won a trophy or two, I think they could have developed the club considerably.

In 1988, Leicester became the first winners of the new

Courage Clubs Championship First Division title. It was interesting that we preceded that successful League campaign, our only Courage League title until our victory in 1995, with a lengthy pre-season tour of Australia and Singapore. I did not make the trip due to police duties at home, but on that three-week tour the team was able to put in some valuable pre-season training and to fine-tune match preparations. It proved very worthwhile, because when my team-mates returned and the season began, we won all of our first seven Courage League games up to Christmas, victories which included a 24–13 defeat of Bath at Welford Road. We had hit the season running, to use a phrase currently in vogue, and it made all the difference. After Christmas, we had only three League games to play, against Orrell, Sale and Waterloo. Orrell hammered us 30–6, we beat Sale 42–15 and then clinched it with a 39–15 win over Waterloo. But the scores themselves illustrate that the Leagues were still very much in their infancy. You don't get many results like that these days in the First Division.

When we were handed the trophy after beating Waterloo, Les Cusworth asked me if I'd like to drop-kick it somewhere. This was hardly tactful at the time, considering I'd just been dropped by England for an incident in which the famous Calcutta Cup was damaged. The side which won that League title was pretty good but it was largely inexperienced. True, we had Les Cusworth, Paul Dodge and Dusty Hare, but apart from them there was not a huge amount of experience, although I suppose Steve Kenney was an exception. But players like Tim Buttimore and Steve Burnhill had a lot of talent, and it was a pity for their sakes and for Leicester's that they never really went on to realize their full potential.

We finished top just ahead of Wasps, our closest challengers, with Harlequins third and Bath fourth on points difference. But the next season we did not defend the title at all effectively, finishing sixth out of twelve, which was our poorest League placing to date. By then, Bath had started their long run of consistency in League rugby and won the title comfortably, although they were to lose out to Wasps for one season after that, 1989–90.

I missed the first five games of that first League season and, due to a series of injuries, ended up playing only sixteen matches in all. Yet I scored ten tries. We must have had an awful lot of scrums on opponents' lines that year! But the year before I had scored twenty tries in twenty matches, which was fair going for a No. 8. I cannot remember most of them, but to see it down in black and white that the second-highest try-scorer for Leicester that season was Rory Underwood with ten would put a nice bright smile on the face of any forward. And in season 1985–6 I scored twenty tries in twenty-six matches.

All those tries – fifty in three seasons – were scored despite my well-known loathing for training, whether it be pre-season or at any stage of the winter. I think it must be rugby's worst-kept secret that I just cannot stand training. I was always a notoriously bad starter to the season, probably because I would do anything to avoid the gruelling pre-season sessions which were more like torture programmes to me. The teams used to go up to Bradgate Park, just north of Leicester on the A50 road, to do some hill running up there – still do, in fact. I used to dread that and would do anything to get out of it. I tried to make it a regular thing that I went down to my first Tigers training session immediately *after* the Bradgate Park experience. It was very, very hard up there. People used to end up being sick, and unless you had done some work previously, which invariably counted me out, you would avoid it like the plague.

People might be surprised at my attitude to training. I fully admit that I have never liked it, rather I have regarded it as a necessary evil to playing the game. But I don't think I am alone in feeling like this – you get the same thing in soccer with certain players, guys who don't like the training yet still put in the performances on a Saturday. It just bores me. The trouble is, there is no competitive element to a training session. If we had a game of five-a-side soccer, for instance, I might enjoy it a bit more because there would be something to win. I hate going into anything knowing I am not able to win.

The arrival of Leagues in English rugby wasn't quite such a culture shock for us at Leicester because we'd had things like the Midlands Merit Table and the John Smith's. While it was always very nice to win those competitions, they were not recognized by the RFU and sometimes you didn't have opponents to relish, like Gloucester, Bristol or Bath, in your league. The arrival of proper Leagues in English rugby brought the top clubs together and structured rugby so that the right clubs played against the right people. It has made the game a lot more competitive and heightened the interest. Before, while you had competitive matches, they were far from the be-all and end-all. If you lost, it didn't cost you anything. These days, every single match can mean an awful lot and the preparation has to be just right.

Handling pressure of that nature, especially when a club as strong and as consistent as Bath is breathing down your neck at the top or setting the pace, is not easy. They have strength in depth, a well of charismatic people ready to slot in when someone drops out. Whatever people say about Leicester, although we have a good side, we don't have the strength in depth we would like. Industry and business are not going as well in this part of the world as they could do and it is not easy for players to come here and get jobs. In the City of London it's a bit easier, and in the west country, where the standard of living is higher than it is here, you have three big centres, Bristol, Bath and Gloucester, all quite close to each other. That helps to bring players into the area.

The season 1994–5 provided the perfect example of Bath's resources. The choice they had at prop was incredible: Victor Ubogu and Dave Hilton, internationals for England and Scotland respectively; John Mallett, who toured South Africa with England in 1994 and was a member of the 1995 World Cup squad, Chris Clark and Darren Crompton. All of them were competing for first-team places and all were being pushed by the club towards higher honours. The back row was another rich seam, with men like John Hall, Ben Clarke, Steve Ojomoh, Andy Robinson and Eric Peters competing for places. I know Peters and Hilton play for Scotland, but as far as English rugby is concerned, I don't believe it is healthy for so much playing talent to be congregated at one club. It might suit Bath, but you can't tell me that Chris Clark is going to develop into an international prop by playing just two or three first-team games a season. Those fringe players must surely move elsewhere if they want to develop to the full and have any chance of fulfilling their international aspirations.

To give Bath their full credit, they have got their act together and are actively recruiting. I think Leicester are starting to get there in this respect, although we are still not as good at it as Bath. Yet perhaps we started a little earlier than Bath, who were clearly in a stage of rebuilding last season. In the mid-eighties, we lost players of the calibre of Paul Dodge, Peter Wheeler, Dusty Hare and Nick Youngs, people it is hard to replace. To lose players of that quality does knock the stuffing out of you and it takes time to regroup. This was very apparent throughout last season, when Bath mounted their campaign without the huge influences of Jack Rowell, Stuart Barnes and Richard Hill in their various roles. But as for payments to players, I have no reason to believe that Bath are resorting to such measures to attract new talent. For all clubs, it is important to find jobs for players, and if someone can use rugby as a way of getting a better job, then why not allow them to do so? I see nothing wrong with that. We at Leicester have to try to match Bath's prowess in this field, not cast aspersions on their methods. You should never criticize others because of their success in a certain direction: you just try harder to match them.

If the Courage Leagues were something of a disappointment for us after that inaugural season, until we won the title for the second time in 1995, that is, then we were at least more successful in the Cup. After losing semi-finals in what was then the John Player Cup to Bath in 1986 and Wasps in 1987, and then going out in the fourth round to Bath in 1988, we reached the Pilkington Cup final in 1989, meeting our old foes Bath once more at Twickenham. It was a match in which we had a good first half, competing very effectively. But Damian Cronin then began to dominate the second-half line-outs for Bath and that gave them the platform they needed. We could manage only two Dusty Hare penalty goals (it was Dusty's last appearance for the club before he retired) which were matched by Stuart Barnes's two for Bath. Bath won it through Barnes's try two minutes from the end of the game when wing Barry Evans took a dummy and stayed out with his man – not an easy decision to make.

I felt Bath were worthy winners because they played much better than us in the second half. It was a pity from our point of view that we had not been able to build on our initial 6–0 lead. John Reason wrote in the *Sunday Telegraph*: 'Richards was his usual Colossus in the loose and although Ian Smith is physically anything but as big as that, he had a hand or a foot in a great deal that was useful, and so did John Wells.' So at least the back row did its bit. But Bath's late score was enough to deny us the Cup.

It was to be four years before we got another chance of banishing the memory of that Cup final defeat. This time, on 1 May 1993, we met Harlequins in the final at Twickenham on a glorious sunny day hot enough for some people to get sunburned. It was Quins' third consecutive final: they had beaten Northampton 25–13 after extra time in 1991 and lost to Bath 15–12, again after extra time, twelve months later. This time, Bath had fallen, astonishingly, at the third-round stage, losing 9–8 to Second Division Waterloo on a day when Stuart Barnes had decided it would be safe to play instead for the Barbarians.

So it came down to us or Quins. We won it 23–16, and if it was not the classic some people had expected, all I can say is that in the conditions it was satisfactory just to win. It was incredibly hot out there and the players became very tired.

Michael Austin, writing in *Rothmans Rugby Union Yearbook*, reported:

> Boot and blunder was the general theme but two Leicester forwards, Richards and Back, rose above the shortcomings. Richards, a powerful mauler, made a significant contribution in the loose and Back, the openside flanker, launched a 65-yard diagonal kick to confirm the depth of his talents, which England have yet to acknowledge. The unassuming Wells, in his last game as captain after two seasons, also played mightily.

A crowd of fifty-four thousand saw the game in which we scored tries through Stuart Potter and Martin Johnson. John Liley converted both and landed two penalties, and Jez Harris dropped a goal. But perhaps our best display had been in the semi-final against Northampton, when we scored twenty-three points before half-time to completely deflate the Saints' challenge. We won 28–6 in the end against a powerful side apparently on its game at that time. It was a very satisfying way to reach a Cup final.

The following year, we were back at Twickenham, having made the long journey in defence of our Pilkington Cup. Just one team stood between us and a successful defence – you guessed it, Bath. If the pundits had been less than thrilled at the spectacle of the 1993 final, then its successor was widely regarded as one of the poorest ever. The critics had a point, too.

It was a very disappointing game which was ruined by the poor weather. It rained constantly, the ball was soaked and slippery and frustration built up for every player on the field. We needed to secure quality ball to release our backs but could never quite manage it. We made too many basic errors, which only increased our frustration. At times, emotions might have boiled over a little too much, but I disagree with those who said that there was an unpleasant undercurrent running throughout the match. I think it was just that certain Bath players were finding it difficult to come to terms with the fact that our pack was at last starting to hold its own and offer a coherent threat to any opposition. Before, we had usually thrived off scraps when we met a powerful pack like Bath's; now, we were starting to create something ourselves and to hold our own up front. People don't always like that, and so it was a very hard physical battle. Sadly, we didn't do ourselves justice. We knew we had to win up front to beat Bath, and we couldn't quite do that. They got the better of us, perhaps most importantly in the area of kidology – they played the referee a lot better than we did.

It was 9–9 at half-time but second-half tries by Swift and Catt took Bath well clear. It finished at 21–9, and it was one of the most disappointing days of my career. Not only had we lost the final, we'd lost our Cup and taken part in a poor game on a lousy day. There wasn't much to take from it in consolation.

The fact is that Bath have an intensity Leicester have not yet matched. It comes partly from a very tight knit community. At Leicester nowadays our players come in from all over the place, whereas at Bath, everyone is much more local and therefore more focused. That influences the feeling they have at the club. It is valuable in terms of creating and building up team spirit to see each other socially quite a lot. It engenders togetherness. Too many Leicester players live too far away from the base of the club, and of course we also lack Bath's strength in depth.

Bath have the connections at higher levels, too. I am disappointed that Leicester player Darren Garforth has not received more recognition from England. Darren has come on enormously as a player and deserves a chance to show what he can do at a higher level. But as for what Leicester can do as a side, all there is to aim for is a relentless tracking of Bath. We have to match the standards they set to win the big trophies. It is a tough task, but the Tigers showed that they are capable of rising to that challenge in winning the League title in 1995, and all the signs are there that they can continue to do so in the future. Our recruitment programme needs to be stepped up, because we must find the quality players to strengthen not just the first team itself but the first-team squad. That is the secret of any successful club. Nothing can be achieved if you don't have replacements of good enough quality to step in.

The 1995 Courage League title triumph was just reward for all the considerable work which had been put in at the club by players, coaches and officials both on and off the field. At one point in the mid to late 1980s, I think Leicester were happy to stay where they were, perhaps not winning League titles but getting along with some good wins over notable opponents. But one turning point came when Tony Russ joined the club, because he immediately showed that he wanted to improve us and get the whole club moving forward in terms of results. That urgency quickly took root in the minds of the players and we went from there.

With Russ's guidance and the spirit of the committee we proved that we could project Leicester Rugby Football Club forward a considerable distance. Yet in spite of everything, the destiny of the League title all came down to one match, the Leicester–Bath clash at Welford Road in April. I think everyone was pretty sure that whoever won that game would go on to become League champions.

That we emerged the victors was extremely pleasing, but Bath gave us a fright. When we led 21–9, I think it was, some people might have thought it was all over. It is never safe to make assumptions where Bath are concerned. Their capacity to strike back was shown with two important scores that had us on edge at 24–21. But thankfully Rory Underwood's late try clinched matters in our favour. Bath's back play was tremendous, and their finishing very clinical. But we deserved to win on the day.

There had, on the other hand, been some days when we had played badly and perhaps did not deserve to come out on top. They say that is a sign of a good side, and perhaps that is true, but it was in many ways an inconsistent season nonetheless.

One of my favourite pastimes: out in the fresh air, tramping the fields looking for a bird or a rabbit for the pot. *(Allsport)*

A major hazard of the job. I often end up having a chat about rugby with a motorist. *(Presse-Sports)*

At work with the Instant Response Unit. *(News Team)*

The most important part of my life: my family. At home with my wife Nicky and daughter Jessica.

Early days: That's me at the bottom in the middle, with my head nearest the trophy.

Some great men of Leicester: Peter Wheeler *(left)* Tony Russ *(above left)* and Les Cusworth *(above)*. Though he isn't pictured here Chalky White, and many others, could certainly be added to any list of Tigers greats.
(Mike Brett/Mike Brett/Allsport)

OPPOSITE PAGE:
(Top) Outjumping Brian Spillane to the line-out ball on my England debut, against Ireland in 1986. I scored two tries that day and will never forget the expression on Peter Winterbottom's face when I ran back after the second! *(Mike Brett)*

(Below) One of the worst moments of my career. Wales beat England to put us out of the 1987 World Cup at the quarter-final stage. *(Mike Brett)*

Training with England, the thing that takes me away from my family so often through the long winter months. *(Allsport)*

Action from England's 1995 Grand Slam season. Getting the ball away against Wales at Cardiff. *(Mike Brett)*

On the charge against Ireland and the fierce wind in the first half in Dublin. *(Allsport)*

Trying to retain possession despite Olivier Roumat's efforts in the French match at Twickenham. *(Allsport)*

I have enjoyed every moment of my time at Leicester – it's a great club. Here I'm keeping an eye on what Wasps might do next. *(Allsport)*

Even before Christmas we knew that the defeat at Bristol would make a large dent in our title hopes. And when we lost at Gloucester, too, it seemed as though that might be the end of them.

The match at Gloucester should never have taken place, in my opinion, for the conditions were atrocious. But what helped us was that in defending their title Bath were also a shade inconsistent by their usual standards, losing the odd point here and there and then being defeated 11–10 at Wasps at the end of March. That opened the door for us, but we still knew we would have to beat them at Welford Road to win the League.

We had drawn 20–20 down at Bath earlier in the season. Tony Underwood got caught up in traffic on the motorway and missed the kick-off, and we had to put a reserve scrum-half, Jamie Hamilton, on the wing and hope against hope that we could somehow manage. When Tony did arrive and quickly got changed, the message came from the bench to tell Jamie to feign some sort of injury so that Tony could get on to the field. But I wasn't having any of that. I told them we would play on with the team we had, because Jamie looked as though he was playing all right. In the end, we equalized through a try by none other than Jamie Hamilton, which somehow seemed to be poetic justice. But it was a poor game in which nobody played very well.

In the season as a whole, then, we took three points out of four off Bath and beat Wasps, usually the next toughest challengers, twice in League matches. I believe those results probably established our right to the title.

Of course, throughout the season, every side had its leading internationals coming and going due to the demands of the international squads. That made it desperately difficult for all the top clubs, but to see unsung heroes like Paul Grant, Bill Drake-Lee, Wayne Kilford and Chris Tarbuck coming into our team and playing so well was a sheer delight. It not only illustrated the growing strength of our overall squad but emphasized Leicester's tremendous spirit. Often, people had not played with their colleagues for as long as four, five or six weeks. Establishing momentum and cohesion in those circumstances is extremely difficult. So I think by the end we won the League fair and square.

As for the future, I think Leicester must face the fact that to consistently win trophies they are going to have to find a way of matching Bath, for I cannot see the west country club losing the plot for long. I believe they will always be strong. In 1994–5 they were perhaps not as good as they have been, especially in the previous season – yet they proved very determined in the defence of their title and in retaining the Pilkington Cup. The loss of Jack Rowell and those key players over the preceding twenty-four months was a factor in their marginal decline in the playing sense. That inner hunger to succeed stays with them, in both good and more difficult times – though Bath don't really have bad times. Once they have integrated the newer players into their set-up, I expect them to go from strength to strength. It's quite possible that they will run away with the League title again in the 1995–6 League season. We are likely to have to improve by as much as 10 per cent just to hang on to our title. We can do that, I believe, because we still have plenty of room for improvement.

One of the great factors in our success was our defence; we tackled ferociously well all season. Up front, Matt Poole played very well, especially in the last few games, when he really came into his own. And between them, Jez Harris and John Liley made sure that we put points on the scoreboard throughout almost all our matches. Jez's ability to drop goals – his total of fourteen for the season equalled his previous best – was a highly valuable weapon in our armour. And when he lost his goal-kicking touch, John Liley was there to step in and kick the goals. Both players were what you might term 'only' good club players, but they did as much as anybody to take us to the title.

Harris is a much under-rated footballer. He got a lot of stick after our Cup semi-final defeat at home against Wasps, but it was totally unjustified. Liley wasn't even in the side at the start of the season – Wayne Kilford was at full-back – but he took his chance when it came and played a major role. Kilford, in fact, returned for our final match to play on the wing when we had to beat Bristol without five internationals. It was that kind of ability to fill in in different roles that was ultimately crucial. The international players who had to watch that vital game from the bench found it a most frustrating experience. In the build-up to the World Cup the England management had limited members of the squad to playing in two League matches in April, and those who had used up their quota had to sit it out. I did not have to agonize about which games to play because injury had kept me out of some matches for Leicester anyway.

We realized that that last game at Welford Road would be very difficult in the absence of so many experienced and talented players. It was some firepower to be without. But the lads who came in played so well that our win was always on the cards. For me, it was an immensely proud moment to be the captain as we lifted the League title after our 17–3 victory. Leicester Rugby Club means everything to me, and to share that great prize with all my friends and team-mates was as good a feeling as I have known.

We spent the summer of 1995 pondering where the club now needs to go to keep making progress. Off the field, building work had already begun by the end of the 1994–5 season, but perhaps we will have to take some hard-nosed decisions about matters on the pitch. If it means having to import some player or players because the lads we have got have been playing to their limit and cannot improve, then we must make that difficult choice and act. Sentiment cannot enter into the equation.

However, I expect our squad to have the same basis as we defend our title. The experience we possess in so many players will be of great value. John Wells, for example, who stepped in as captain last season when I was injured, once again did a tremendous job. He and I are now known as Tweedledee and Tweedledum around Welford Road. There's gratitude for you!

I'd like to round up this chapter by discussing one regular fixture each year. In some people's eyes, it might not seem to have the attraction, excitement or challenge that a Cup final or critical League game would hold, but in my opinion the annual post-Christmas game against the Barbarians is something that illustrates all that is good about rugby. All Leicester folk hold this traditional fixture in high esteem. Perhaps, to some outside observers, the day of the Barbarians has passed. Certain people try to write obituaries for the Baa-baas, claiming that rugby today is too important for such a club. The matches the Barbarians play, they seem to suggest, no longer mean anything.

In my view the Barbarians are needed just as much today, if not more. Rugby has become a very serious sport, but is it good for the game if *every* match is played and prepared for with such intensity? Do we have to have that pressure at all levels everywhere the game is played? I, for one, certainly hope not. Barbarians rugby provides a release from that pressure, an opportunity to indulge oneself and to play a match purely for pleasure – the enjoyment of the game itself and of attempting to produce some fine, open rugby, and the pleasure of meeting people socially whom you might only have met before on the rugby pitch and getting to know them better.

Our match against the Barbarians each December is a unique occasion and it is something we hope will continue for ever. The Barbarians are respected throughout the world because of the type of game they play and their attitude to rugby. At Leicester we are honoured that they come and play us. It is certainly one of the highlights, if not the highlight, of our year.

Even if the League programme intrudes even further into such traditions, we will still keep the Barbarians fixture. That week, if necessary, the first team will just have to play two matches, one a League game and the other against the Barbarians. And despite the problems the Barbarians sometimes have in raising the kind of side which was once possible, they can still put together a pretty powerful combination to meet us. Of course, some of their teams have been better than others in recent years, but at the end of the day almost all of them are international class. I just hope that English rugby understands that there is a place in the game for the Baa-baas and allows people the flexibility to be available to play for them. In an amateur game, I believe it is essential for players to be able to continue to exercise their right to represent an invitation team such as the Barbarians if they wish to.

We have had some outstanding games against the Barbarians at Leicester. I played them for the first time in December 1982, when the Tigers won 36–16 against, in the words of Martin Johnson in the *Leicester Mercury*, 'a side that, potentially, contained fifteen British Lions'. Martin summed up this fixture perfectly:

> If the Christmas holiday doesn't do it, there is always the Leicester Tigers–Barbarians match to intoxicate the senses and yesterday's epic at Welford Road produced eighty minutes of spell-binding rugby. With eighteen thousand people packed inside the ground and plenty locked out of it, Tigers produced some magnificent rugby to provide coach Chalkie White with the perfect farewell present. Led with eye-popping commitment from captain Steve Johnson and inspired by a virtuoso performance from fly-half Les Cusworth, Tigers ran in five tries to two.

The following year, Leicester won 30–26 against a Barbarians side which was formidably strong up front. It is never any use picking great backs without the forwards of sufficient calibre to win them the ball, and that year the Barbarians arrived with a huge pack containing players like Maurice Colclough and Steve Bainbridge, Phil Blakeway, Ike Stephens, Peter Winterbottom and the Agen hooker Bernard Dupont. Those forwards gave us plenty to think about! Also in that team were the New Zealanders Andy Donald at scrum-half and Craig Green at centre, Welsh fly-half maestro Gareth Davies, plus Bernard Vivies who, sadly for him, had a very unfortunate game. Poor Vivies – Martin Johnson was moved to comment: 'He is to full-back play what foot and mouth is to cattle.'

It was a very hard physical game, far from the popular image of Barbarians rugby, which some seem to think only means throwing the ball around the field for eighty minutes. It wasn't like that at all that day. Instead, we had a real hard test and we enjoyed it hugely. In 1984 we gave a Barbarians side which included seven Welsh internationals their biggest-ever hiding in the fixture, 35–11. I managed to score one of our six tries that day, my first against the Baa-baas. I will always regard that as a proud moment. However, a year later, the invitation side had its revenge, winning 19–16. A look at the Barbarians forward line-up might reveal how determined they were to win the match – front row: Whitefoot and Phillips of Cardiff, Pearce of Northampton; locks: Colclough and Dooley; back row: Winterbottom, Leslie and Pickering. Behind them, the Bath half-back pairing of Barnes and Hill, plus Hugo MacNeill, Mark Titley, Simon Halliday, Ieuan Evans and Arthur Emyr, provided no small measure of icing upon the cake.

In 1986, we led the Baa-baas 12–0 but somehow managed to lose 18–22 against a side that included some magnificent players – Carling and the Frenchman Denis Charvet at centre, Rob Andrew and Robert Jones at half-back and a strongly Irish-flavoured forward pack. In 1987 we more than made up for that by scoring nine tries in a 48–30 win which celebrated in appropriate fashion the birth of Les Cusworth's second child in the early hours of that morning. Jonathan Davies and Robert Jones were in tandem as the visiting half-backs that day, helping to create their side's four tries. The next year we lost the fixture heavily, by 36–19, and went down again in both 1990 and 1991. So although there was one more recent match for which the Barbarians struggled to raise as strong a side as usual, there is hardly a case to be made for Leicester to pull out because it is always a walkover. Very far from it. And look at the pleasure the fixture has brought to Tigers supporters. In recent seasons, we have seen world-class stars like Serge Blanco, Philippe Sella,

David Campese, Jonathan Davies, Robert Jones and all manner of other people at Welford Road. You cannot write off all that tradition, glamour and success simply by saying it's time to do other things. The crowds still pour in for the game and long may it remain so. I for one have gained enormous pleasure from being involved in these matches over the years, and I hope to be able to do so for several years yet to come.

4 A Town Called Roanne

'Roanne, sub-prefecture of the Loire, industrial town (weaving and metallurgy) of 44,518 inhabitants on the left bank of the Loire at the commencement of the canal from Roanne to Digoin.'

The old guidebook I dug out sketched some faraway town to which I had never been in a country I could hardly say I knew well, apart from the odd school and holiday trip and from leafing through school books. The town did not seem to have too much going for it. The above words, from Nagel's *Guide Bleu* to France, were written in 1949, not long after the end of the Second World War. But when I got to Roanne I found that not very much had changed in the intervening years. It is not in the Alps or the Massif Central; it's neither here nor there, really. It's a town of about the same size as Hinckley and it is run on very similar lines. It's a close family community where everybody knows everybody else's business.

Roanne is in an area few British tourists would know well. Lyons, much the biggest city of the region, is about fifty miles to the east; Vichy, where the French government of that name had its headquarters in the war, a similar distance to the west. Clermont-Ferrand, the club of the 1995 French rugby captain Philippe Saint-André, is a little further to the south-west and to the south lies the industrial town of St Etienne, famous for its soccer team. It is not a region renowned as a destination for British holidaymakers, yet it would be familiar to lots of British people through the fame of the nearby Beaujolais vineyards.

So how did I come to be heading off from my home in the English midlands to a town somewhere in the middle of France? Well, my father used to be involved with Nuneaton Rugby Club and we had a lot of ties there. One of Dad's friends in Nuneaton had spent some time in France and had played rugby over there. He suggested to my parents that I ought to go over for a while; it would help my French, which I had studied at school, he said, and also improve my outlook on rugby.

I am pleased to say that I have always been very close to my parents and still am. All families are different, and I know that by the time they are seventeen or eighteen, some people cannot wait to escape the family home and head off on their own. I was not like that. I got on with my parents and I had a very happy childhood. Our life might have been a simple one but I didn't mind that. I like a calm lifestyle in which time can be found to pursue pleasures and develop friendships.

I have one sister, Adelle, who is a year older than I am. We've always been close, although I don't see as much of her as I'd like as she now lives in Somerset with her husband and two children. My sister and I were together a lot and confided in each other. As a family we'd do the usual things, such as go on picnics and visits, and Adelle and I went on a few French exchanges together when we were at school.

One day the harmony was briefly disturbed. It was while we had a French schoolboy staying with us at home on a school exchange programme. Adelle and I had had an argument – I can't remember now what it was about – and as she went to close a door I pushed it back. Somehow, quite by accident, she managed to put her arm through the plate glass in the door. As soon as I saw the blood I felt terrible, and watching her going off to hospital, where she had around twenty stitches in the arm, did not make me feel any better. I think I apologized, even though it had been an accident. I'm sure Adelle didn't hold it against me for very long, if at all. She has a very nice nature.

When we were in our teens, Adelle and I would go and have a drink together or with our friends and it was always a good feeling to get along so well with your own sister. When I went out with my Dad, who was a draughtsman, it was often to go and watch him play rugby. My mother used to like to entertain, so there were always a lot of people coming round for dinner. We were allowed to stay up sometimes and I suppose seeing and being with grown-ups helped me to mature quickly myself.

My parents have always been wonderfully supportive. Strict, yes – in the traditional fashion – but very fair. My mother was generally more strict than my father, and you might receive a gentler hearing from Dad if you'd done something wrong. But there was never the slightest doubt in my mind that they both loved us dearly and we felt similarly towards them. The example they set me has proved valuable now that I have a family of my own. I have my priorities sorted out and my family is beyond doubt the most important thing in my life.

One of my hobbies is playing cards. I got that from my mum, who was a keen cards player. When I was about twelve or thirteen, I used to go to whist drives with her. I was the only kid there, apart from one girl, Julie Payne. We used to play cards with and against the adults and soon learned all the games.

I went on my first school foreign-exchange programme, to Albertville in France, when I was twelve. I spent two weeks over there and thoroughly enjoyed it. After that I went twice to Albertville and twice to Rouen, while still at school. Those trips planted the seeds of an interest in foreign countries.

It wasn't until I was eleven that I first played rugby, at St Martin's High School in Stoke Golding, near Hinckley. There were two teachers at the school who were especially interested in rugby – Ian Proud and Viv Abrahams. The school was a convent school, and when we played on a Saturday the nuns used to come out to watch us.

I had no interest in the game before that. I was enjoying soccer at junior school and saw no reason to take up rugby. I was like any other soccer-mad child – I wanted to be a centre forward who scored the goals. Doesn't every youngster? As it turned out, I was more effective as a goalkeeper than anywhere else on the field, so a goalie I became. I can't remember the sides I played in actually winning anything, but I went for trials with either Leicester West Under-9s or Under-10s, I forget which. I did not get picked as goalkeeper because I made one fatal mistake.

In one trial game, a particularly large tree laden with conkers caught my eye and proved a strong distraction. Like any typical nine-year-old boy, I was into conkers in a big way and thought that this was too good an opportunity to miss, especially as the tree was just behind our goal. I thought that if I nipped around the goal when play was at the other end, I could pick up some big ones and still have time to run back into position on the goal-line. This was not as daft as it might sound because the opposition did not score once that day. But the selectors saw me scampering off to the conker tree to fill my pockets and clearly took a dim view of it. Not surprisingly, I was not asked to another trial. I expect they thought I lacked the proper attitude.

It's funny, really, because to this day, I still very much like soccer, but I don't think it can match rugby for the sportsmanship which I still believe exists in our game. In soccer, there are too many cheap shots, too many fouls, far too many people diving around trying to get free kicks, whereas in rugby, such things very rarely happen. Of course, there are exceptions to every rule, but in general, I prefer people who play rugby to those who play soccer.

I might have been into football but my father still used to play rugby in those days. Dad was great – he never put any pressure on me to take up the game he enjoyed. He always said to me, 'You play what you like and when you want to.' So I used to go down to Nuneaton Rugby Club with him from time to time; not every Saturday, but just when I fancied it. He wouldn't drag me all over the country to watch games unless I really wanted to go. I suppose I was very young when I first saw a game at Nuneaton, and remember it as a very social, family-orientated occasion.

I remember my father getting up on a Sunday morning, groaning from the bumps and bruises. He didn't get much sympathy from Mum – she would give him some stick if he couldn't do the jobs around the house on a Sunday because he was suffering from the previous day's game. By that time he was getting on a bit, in his late thirties, and shouldn't really have been playing for Nuneaton first team anyway, so he had only himself to blame.

I stopped playing soccer altogether when I left high school and went to John Cleveland College. I was about thirteen by then. From then on, it was all rugby. We'd won the County Cup at St Martin's and at John Cleveland we won it again, though at a different age group, of course. One of my team-mates in that successful side at John Cleveland was Barry Evans, who, like me, was later to become a Tiger. And as well as representing one of England's greatest clubs, we both became full internationals for England.

At St Martin's, I started off in the No. 8 position and then played centre, wing forward, hooker and finally second row in my final years at John Cleveland. It was only when I went to France to play, that I reverted to No. 8. Centre was a bit of an unlikely choice – I think it was just a phase the teacher was going through at the time. Perhaps he was influenced by David Duckham, the England hero – I was blond like David, so maybe he thought I was a future side-stepping genius, though I must say it never occurred to me that I possessed the right qualities. Of all the positions I played around that time, I'd say second row was the worst. No wonder the second-row boys are called the donkeys. They've always got their heads stuck up somebody's backside, always pushing and shoving. They don't get out and do all the nice easy touches, the flash stuff. And considering all the hard work they do hidden away in the forwards, they don't really get the recognition or limelight they probably deserve.

But in those days I was only toying with the game in a very casual manner. I certainly didn't have grand dreams of one day running out for England at Twickenham. That did not seem remotely likely, and such thoughts would have appeared altogether too grandiose.

For a brief spell I went over to Nuneaton on Sundays for mini-rugby at Under-12 or Under-13 age group, but I didn't like that and soon gave it up. Playing on a Saturday was enough for me. I wanted to do other things on a Sunday. Devoting my entire weekend to rugby was not my idea of fun.

My father probably despaired of me from around the age of thirteen to eighteen. All I really enjoyed was rugby, once I had discovered the game relatively late in the day. I didn't do anything out of the ordinary at school because I was basically lazy. The only thing I liked was sport. I used to hang around at home when I wasn't at school, watching videos or working on a scooter my dad had bought to restore. I enjoyed that and was so laid back about schoolwork that I didn't worry. I am sure my parents did, though. I suppose you could say I did a little bit of work at French and I quite liked Physics, but I didn't think much of the rest, although I ended up with seven O-levels. I think I had failed my A-levels before I even sat them because I was skiving off school so much.

By that time I knew I was going to go to France for a prolonged visit and I didn't do much work for my A-levels. In the back of my mind I was a little concerned about my future because jobs were starting to get harder to find for school leavers. But it wasn't enough to make me take anything other than rugby really seriously. In the end, I was skiving off school at least once a week but my parents only found out for sure when I was caught by one of the teachers going into rugby training after school when I hadn't been there during the day. By the time I finally left school, I had improved my rugby a great deal. I wish I could have said the same for my Mathematics and History!

So it came about that I left school in the midlands at seventeen and a half, and just before my eighteenth birthday, drove down to France with my parents. They were going on holiday and it was decided that on the way they would take me to Roanne and get me settled in.

There were, I suppose, mixed feelings in my mind as we boarded the ferry and sailed across the English Channel. I enjoy living in England and always have done. Although I have toured all over the world, and am extremely grateful to rugby for having given me the chance to see so much of other countries, I don't begin to pretend that I am not happiest in my own environment. I like spending time with my family, doing my work and being at home. I am not a globetrotter who yearns to jump on and off aeroplanes at the drop of a hat.

Nevertheless, I recognized that this was a great opportunity to see France and to really learn the language. Living in a country on your own also makes you grow up pretty quickly, because you have to stand on your own feet. There is no turning to others for constant advice or decisions. This was not my first-ever trip to France – I had been on those school exchanges, spending a week or two with French students, and there had been the summer holidays there with my parents, both of whom are great Francophiles, but nothing very long. So this was to be the first big adventure of my life. I didn't know quite what to expect, but I was aware that I had been sheltered, living at home with my parents. It was time to see what the world had to offer and how I might be able to handle it.

The first thing I had to handle, upon our arrival in Roanne, was being greeted by a bunch of cockroaches scurrying about the floor of the apartment the club had arranged for me to stay in. It was not the most endearing of welcomes to what the travel writers call la Belle France. I am not squeamish, but I have to say that the apartment was pretty ordinary and far from clean and I wasn't altogether happy about staying there. My parents agreed and we simply said no. That gave the Roanne Rugby Club officials a problem. In the end, it was decided that I would stay at the home of one of the rugby men while the club found another apartment for me. It seemed a suitable compromise, and so for the next two weeks I shared his home. The club then produced a much nicer apartment and I moved in.

Of course, I had to speak French the whole time, because no one at the club seemed to understand much English. That is hard at first, but it certainly makes you concentrate on the language. And I got by. I discovered that it takes quite a while to improve on your schoolboy French, even when you are thrown in at the deep end. When you start everything comes in a rush, and you learn new words all the time. But then you hit a bit of a plateau and you are quite content to stay at that level. I suppose it is human nature to seek the easy way out.

In 1995 there may well be people who believe that any player who goes abroad to play rugby in another country is greeted with bags of gold coins. My experience was rather different. The club arranged the apartment for me and also fixed me up with a job, nothing else. If I needed money, as quite obviously I would, I would have to work for it. No one was going to subsidize an 18-year-old English lad who was virtually unknown in his own country as a rugby player, never mind France. So I began work at a transport company whose factory was situated on the banks of the Loire. I worked there for the first two or three months loading and unloading lorries.

Then I went cleaning buses for a while, but I didn't find that an immensely rewarding occupation and asked to change. A few weeks later, I went back to the transport company and started going out on deliveries with the drivers as a cabbie's mate. Later, I joined the Citroën factory in Roanne, which specialized in making the engines for those 2CV6 cars which seem so synonymous with provincial France. I was given the task of lifting engines off the conveyer belt, boxing them up and putting stickers on the boxes. I didn't stay there for too long because I didn't get on with some members of the workforce.

Doing a manual job brought me into a section of society which was, let's say, rather interesting. I remember reading a story around that time of the Israeli football player, Avi Cohen, who went to Liverpool. Apparently he was like I was in France, anxious to learn the local language. Unfortunately, some practical jokers seriously misled him on the refinements of the Queen's English. I gather that some of the players convinced him that certain four-letter words were part and parcel of colloquial English. Eventually he had to be taken aside and told very kindly but firmly that such words should not be used in company. He must have wondered why the tea ladies at Anfield always looked so shocked.

Well, I experienced something similar in France. My problem was that the language I was learning in these surroundings was all slang. Sometimes I would be invited to dinner parties and I would express myself in words I had learned on the factory floor. I remember at one, there was an awful silence for a moment; you could almost hear the intake of breath of some of the French women. They would also look at me strangely, and when I asked what was wrong, they would explain delicately what I had said. Of course, I was hugely embarrassed. I'd say, 'I am sorry, but that is what I have been taught.' What I understood to be quite normal vocabulary had turned out to include some appalling swearwords. Looking back, I can see the funny side of it, but it was very awkward at the time.

My attitude to France was that I was there to enjoy myself and to try to further my rugby career. But if I had known then what I know now, I think I could have pushed for a lot more. There was a great deal of money floating around in French rugby, and I could have asked for much more than I got in terms of facilities. The club did promise to give the players a lump sum of money. To start with, this was going to be handed over at Christmas; then it was put off until the end of the season. I asked whether this payment was for expenses and they looked puzzled. 'No, each player gets a lump sum,' they said. Fair enough, I thought. But to this day I have never seen the colour of Roanne's money. They kept coming up with excuses to delay parting with it. This was 1981, but even then rumours were going around as to the money some players in France were earning. It was said to be normal at most clubs to receive fifty pounds a game, but I never saw any of it. I don't know whether the other players at Roanne received anything.

Overall, I'd say that the standard of rugby at the club was poor, but there were a few players who had clearly been rather useful in their earlier days. The thing about French rugby is that because people are paid, as soon as they become worthless in the top flight they go to a second-division club and get a little money there. Then, when they're no longer up to scratch there either, they join a third-division club and earn a bit less there, rather than playing for the reserves at a first- or second-division club and getting nothing financially. There were some guys at Roanne who had played a decent standard of rugby and it was quite an experience to play with them. I alternated between the second row and No. 8. I knew the second-row position from my schooldays, but I didn't really mind where I played.

The strength of our team was in the pack, but the individuals who played there were of very mixed ability and experience. One prop, Robert Papau, had played first-division rugby in his time; another forward ran the local bookshop. But as a unit, we had enough bulk and strength to win plenty of ball in most games. The backs were a little haphazard. The club had brought in a couple of lads from Paris, one of them a fly-half who stood 6ft 4ins tall and weighed a colossal 18 stone! He couldn't run very well, but if kicking was required, he was yer man, as the Irish might say. He would leather the ball vast distances down-field, gaining us huge amounts of territory in a single stroke.

The trouble was, when we did run the ball, we would do strange things. If we got into an attacking position, we would tend to kick it — even from around the opposition 22. Conversely, if we were in deep defence, a real no-hope situation, you could bet your last centime that our brave boys would run the ball as though their lives depended on it. And very often, against all the odds and the complete misgivings of we forwards, it could come off and one of the backs would score a remarkable try.

The rugby at Roanne might not have been exceptional in

terms of class, but in the league of violence it was like most French rugby used to be – right at the top. Our side never actually practised setting people up – and by that I mean going out deliberately to hurt opponents – but some clubs did. Players in our team told us how, at other clubs, they would rehearse such tactics as, for example, when an opponent stuck his head through at a line-out, grabbing and holding on to his arms while a colleague went round the side to give him a good smack in the chops. A lot of kicking of people goes on too. This didn't happen at all French clubs, of course, but it did show me another side to the game and I was left with the distinct impression that the French rugby scene is undeniably a violent one. It is just the way the French are: they are a very temperamental people and if you get a hard Frenchman, you get a hard man. And yet at the same time the players are very carefree: even in a big league match, they'd think nothing of launching attacks from behind their own goal-line. It's all part of their make-up; they do it at all levels.

About seven weeks after I joined Roanne, two other English recruits arrived. Both were from Crewe and Alsager College, and both were quite good players. Peter Evans was a wing forward who hailed from Moseley, and Peter McKenna, a centre, came from the north-east. I was pleased to have them around. They were given living accommodation in apartments occupied chiefly by the Algerians and Arabs who had come to the town in search of employment and settled there. In England, our culture is geared towards ownership of houses, but in France, many more people have apartments, and the Algerians and Arabs tended to have a little quarter to themselves.

I'd go round and spend time quite often with the two Peters. We had good times and some fun parties. I was already meeting lots of people through my job as a cabbie's mate, being out on the road most days and stopping off at various places. At each collection or unloading point there would be a fridge and the driver, my 'mate', would open a bottle of beer. As we might make nine or ten stops during the course of a day, he usually drove home back to the depot with nine or ten beers inside him, but he thought nothing of driving having drunk so much.

If this habit made me raise my eyebrows, then I was amazed at the way the locals carried the drinking culture through to their rugby. They would think nothing of having a glass of wine before going out to play a game, and this attitude extends right up to the very top of the French game. Two or three seasons ago, when the famous Paris team Racing Club de France reached the French club championship final at the Parc des Princes, they had an assistant carry out a tray of champagne, which they sipped during the half-time interval. They won the championship, incidentally. I am not in the habit of quaffing wine either during or before matches, in case you haven't noticed. In fact, I never even eat before playing, apart from breakfast. I find it very difficult to eat anything at lunchtime. The French, though, would sit down to a pre-match meal of roast beef, mashed potatoes, beans and a glass of wine. I still find it incredible when I look back that they could do this without suffering any adverse effect. But they loved it.

On the other hand, our hosts could never understand why we three English lads would want to go out on a Friday or Saturday night for a few drinks as part of our social scene. With a game to play on a Sunday, they thought this was extraordinary behaviour. But for the English it is a tradition to go out on those nights, and we saw no harm in it. It was not as if we were coming in drunk at four o'clock in the morning or anything like that. If we had a good few drinks on a Friday night, we'd lie in late on Saturday morning and take it pretty easy on Saturday night. By Sunday morning we were as fresh as daisies again. But the club wasn't very keen on it and told us so. My view was that I wasn't being paid a penny to play for them so, within reason, I would do what I wanted.

We three Englishmen might not have been able to eat roast beef before matches, but like our fellow countrymen we were quickly nicknamed 'Les Rosbifs'. After the conviviality of the pre-match arrangements we were all fascinated to see how the

French went about their after-match social activities. Because the French grounds are owned by the municipalities, they do not have clubhouses as such on site. So Roanne officials and supporters would set up perhaps half a dozen tables at the back of the main stand (with umbrellas if it was raining) and get out the bottles of Pernod, over which the players would have a good chat with some of their supporters. There was, I noted, very little communication between the home team and the opposition. After that, on a typical evening after a home game, we would move on to a café somewhere nearby and carry on drinking. Then we would have a meal, either at the café or at some local restaurant, and head for a nightclub. If we were playing away, we would break our journey at a roadside café or inn and have dinner. I used to enjoy some of those trips, travelling back and stopping off for a meal somewhere where the big winter log fire would be crackling on the hearth and the food was like the people of the region, hearty. It also meant that I got to see places I'd probably never have come across by myself.

Roanne rugby club set out intending to win promotion from third division to the second in the season I was there. The crowds which supported us were pretty small, usually around six hundred with a thousand maximum for an important game, but you could not accuse the club of failing to provide entertainment for those who did turn up. The match against Digoin, the nearest town to Roanne, was apparently always a strongly contested derby. The day I played against my adopted club's great rivals, the game ended up in such a mass brawl that spectators were jumping over the perimeter fence to get involved in the fighting! I have to say it was one of the most extraordinary sights I have ever seen in rugby. Our touch-judge, Pierre Reycaud, got himself sent off and banned from the line for the rest of the game for hitting someone over the head with his flagpole. It really was quite farcical. I stood there watching all this going on and just couldn't believe my eyes. Normally, you would be in there helping your friends, but I was so astounded that I didn't do a thing. Among the many supporters who ran on to the pitch to swap punches was a little old lady who hit the referee over the head with her brolly. It was absolutely unbelievable, but it did happen.

Most people in rugby will know that I am not one for violence in the game. Of course, my experience as a police officer under-lines in my mind the need to behave at all times and not to get involved in such situations unless it is absolutely unavoidable. But as a rookie at Roanne I did get caught up in an incident which illustrates the violent streak which ran through French rugby at that time. I cannot remember so many years later the precise match, but I do recall what happened pretty clearly. I had gone down to retrieve a loose ball and was stuck at the bottom of a group of bodies. But my head was clear and I could see what was going on. Suddenly, I saw this opponent come running towards the pile-up and the next thing I knew I was watching his boot crash into my face, breaking my nose and splattering it all over my face.

Keeping your temper under control is, of course, an integral part of the game, one of the many disciplines Rugby Union requires. But as an 18-year-old lad, I had probably not yet acquired the kind of discipline which I now expect of myself. When I was able to crawl out of the mass of bodies, I stood up, angrily focused on my assailant and landed a punch flush on his jaw which sent him down like a log. For that, I was pulled aside by the referee and immediately sent off. To this day, it remains the only dismissal of my entire playing career. This one blot on my copybook is a matter of regret to me: I never wanted to be sent off the rugby field for foul play, or for any other reason, for that matter.

By the time I got to the side of the field, the enormity of what I had done started to sink in. Trouble with the English, the locals were doubtless saying as they shook their heads. But although I'm not trying to excuse my retaliation, I did take considerable exception to such premeditated, unjustified viol-ence. I could not see why someone should get away with doing what this player had done.

There were some animated conversations among our club officials that night about what sentence I might receive. I didn't have a clue as to the going rate, as it were, but I duly got notice a week or two later that my case was to be heard by a local committee. I volunteered to turn up and explain what had happened, but I was advised that they probably wouldn't be able to understand what I was talking about anyway, so I didn't bother. The verdict was that I had been suspended for eight matches, which seemed to me an awfully long time.

If I was baffled by the severity of the sentence, given I had seen what seemed to pass for normal behaviour on French rugby fields, I was just as puzzled by the attitude of the Roanne club official who told me the news. He didn't seem overly concerned, and when I inquired why, he said simply: 'It is for eight friendly matches. You can play in all the league matches, the important ones.' Thank goodness for French justice! The referee's report of this thoroughly unsavoury incident was the cause of some amusement at Roanne. Apparently, he had called me 'the Beast' for what I had done. I didn't know whether to feel proud or ashamed of such a title!

I have to say that I was very rarely attacked by the opposition. In spite of my youth, my team-mates did not make any special effort to shield me that I was aware of. I think the reason no one ever really had a go at me apart from on that one occasion was that the opposing teams probably thought that at my age I was not too much of a threat. It was probably not until the end of a game, by which time it was too late, that they might have realized I had actually played pretty well. By the end of my time at Roanne, I was just as much a man as my team-mates. You had to grow up very quickly in French rugby. It is certainly not a place for the faint-hearted.

The French have a very different attitude to home and away games. They seem to think that if you are playing at home you must win every game, but that the results of away matches don't really matter too much. It is almost as if they write off any away games before they even start the journey. Of course, if they do manage an away win then that is a cause for celebration, but it clearly doesn't mean as much as the home game in front of your own supporters. The French international side have thought this way for many years and lots of international players regard them as different players, performance-wise, in Paris from anywhere else. Whether the victories of the French national side under Pierre Berbizier in the two Tests on their New Zealand tour in 1994 heralds a change in that tradition remains to be seen.

I saw a little of the local area beyond Roanne. One weekend, the two Peters and I organized a trip up into the Jura mountains to see the former England international Nigel Horton, who was coaching a club named Saint Claude up in the Alps, very close to the Swiss border. It was absolutely gorgeous up there – wonderfully clean, fresh air with the tang of winter cold, but often there was bright sunlight and everything had a clean feel to it. Nigel had originally left England to go and play for the famous Stade Toulouse club and to run a bar in that city. As his playing days drew to a close, he agreed to join Saint Claude. When we visited him in this delightful part of the world I could fully understand his decision.

There was plenty of snow to be seen, of course, where Nigel was, and in winter even around Roanne there used to be snow sometimes on the hills behind the town. Occasionally, we would try to go skiing but it was pretty perilous. We would be trying to ski downhill on cross-country skis, which is not only very difficult but extremely dangerous. We never got far before ending up in a pile of snow.

Roanne might have been only a third-division club but there was nothing third rate about their facilities. They were superb. In France, the local council gives each club a sum of money each year to finance its operation. The further up the playing ladder you go, the more money you are given. And the fact that the councils own the grounds frees the clubs from having to worry about fund-raising, which is a constant source of concern at most English clubs. The system used in France takes a lot of pressure off clubs to stay afloat. They certainly haven't got as many worries as their counterparts in England.

Roanne played at a very nice stadium whose playing surface was incredible. They shared it with the local soccer club, so you could be sure it was always going to be rolled very well every time they cut it. The pitch was seldom very hard because it was well watered. It was also extremely level and the grass was nice and short. It was a real pleasure to play on, nothing like the heavy, muddy pitches you encounter in England at clubs like Bath and Bristol during a wet winter. I just wish clubs over here could manage a similar standard for their playing surfaces.

The Roanne soccer team was then in the second division of the national league – a very reasonable level – and so the rugby team also benefited from brilliant facilities. The changing rooms were good and there was a training pitch at the back and a swimming pool next to the stadium. You couldn't fault it. I used to look at these first-class facilities and have to remind myself that this wasn't an Agen, a Toulouse or a Grenoble – all this magnificence was for a third-division club. And this was fifteen years ago. Even today, English clubs cannot boast such facilities at their disposal. Furthermore, the thing about France is that virtually wherever you go, you find facilities of a similar quality. Béziers, once the mightiest club in all France, have now fallen upon hard times and have lost their position of eminence, but if you look at the wonderful new stadium which was built for them by the local authorities, you realize how much support rugby clubs get across the Channel. It really is another world.

That season Roanne were pushing for promotion until very near the end of the programme. But then we lost to a couple of teams, one of which was Villefranche, a thoroughly useful side. Their team featured a former French international who had moved down divisions. They beat us 13–3, I think it was, after a particularly hard game which included an almighty fight. Our prop, Robert Papau, had his nose broken. It was a do-or-die game from our point of view: we were near the top of the table but needed to win to maintain our hopes of promotion.

Unfortunately, that defeat, closely followed by another, ended our prospects of going up.

In the French system the first, second and third divisions are sub-divided so that teams from the same area play each other. Then the top two of each play each other and they work out promotion from there. The benefit of playing regionally at this level was that the furthest we ever travelled was to the other side of Lyons, about a hundred miles away to somewhere like Bourg.

Overall, I would say that I got on very well with nearly everyone in Roanne. When the founder of Guillerman Transport, where I'd worked when I first arrived in the town, died, I was rather surprised to be among those invited to his funeral a few days later. It was held in a little village just outside Roanne and turned out to be one of the best funerals I have ever been to, if you can describe a funeral in those terms. Everyone was down at the local café drinking, hundreds of people were there and it went on all day long. Everybody said it was the way he would have wanted it, and I regarded it as an honour to be invited and to be given such a warm welcome.

In France people are a lot more relaxed about things than we are. In rugby, they don't sit down and watch endless videos to try to identify some imagined weakness in the team they are about to play. Both rugby and life in general are very laid back – what happens happens, and I must admit I quite liked that. The preparatory stuff for matches all goes over their heads just as it often goes over mine, too.

Nevertheless, by March, ten months after joining Roanne, I decided that I wanted to leave. The other two English players had already gone home, and it became increasingly clear to me that despite optimistic words and promises, there was not going to be any financial reward – not at Christmas, not in April and not at the end of the season, either. It never looked like materializing. The experience had certainly transformed my French, but the language I took home with me was fairly colloquial, to put it politely, which was something of a pity. The people with whom I lived and worked were basic and earthy and they used basic language a lot of the time. Even so, I still learned a lot and made some good friendships.

Looking back, the only regret I have is that I was so young when I went to France. I was too young, really, to appreciate the social opportunities – I was quite shy and in many ways I kept myself to myself. It was due to inexperience: I was not used to life on my own or to mixing with large numbers of people I had never met before. I hope the locals did not consider the young Englishman in their midst in any way arrogant, because it certainly was not that. I was just young and shy, and that was all that prevented me from mixing more.

I was a little lonely sometimes: if you are used to coming home to a family it is quite a strange feeling opening the door to an empty apartment in a strange land. It's the little things that you notice, like just having a chat about your day. It's not something of which you are aware until it's not there any more. I missed that probably more than anything, and in the end that is why I came home. It is the same for anyone who goes to live overseas on their own, but the problem is intensified when you don't speak the language well.

In such a club and in such a region, on the edge of the Beaujolais wine area, it would have been nice to have made some contacts. If I were to go back there now and play I would establish a much wider circle of friends than I managed to do last time. In the end, I came home because I had got into a bit of a rut. The team was not going to achieve its aim of promotion and all my money had been spent. The thought of joining the police force was already strongly in my mind and I decided that this option would offer me a much brighter career path than hanging around in France for another year or so. I had not received any offers to go elsewhere and I don't really think I would have accepted them even if there had been any. My mind was set upon coming home. I had enjoyed my time with Roanne but it was time to leave, and I did so on good terms with the club. They were basically very nice people.

I still love France as a country. In fact, when I returned to England and my parents' house, in many ways I missed it. But I think France has changed in recent years, and not for the better. There are too many English people living over there and the French have catered too much for them, presenting menus and signs and so on in English. If you go to some places in the country now, you find yourself tripping over English visitors and residents. I think that is a shame. At least when I was there what I did see was probably the real France before it became overrun with English people, although I doubt very much that Roanne itself has been invaded by les Anglais.

5 England's Rugby Renaissance

Any glance at a record of my international career will reveal some alarming gaps in my England appearances at certain periods. In many cases injuries have been to blame, but there have also been other reasons for my exclusion.

Perhaps the most controversial came in 1992, just as England were preparing to meet South Africa in an international for the first time in eight years. Twickenham was finishing its latest round of rebuilding work and the new East Stand was to be open for the first time. The international against Canada earlier that autumn had been staged in the very unusual venue of Wembley Stadium because of the construction work at Twickenham. That was a unique match, and I was pleased to be a part of it. I thought I'd done quite well, too, playing a solid part in England's victory by 26–13. But unbeknownst to me, the selectors had asked for a special video following me through the entire match. A camera was trained on absolutely everything I did. If this was Big Brother watching, it certainly had a major effect on my career: I was not to play another game for England for a whole year. Geoff Cooke announced the team to meet South Africa at the Petersham Hotel on a training weekend and when he left my name off the list, I was shocked. To say I was disappointed would be the understatement of the season. As soon as the team had been announced, we went off to Twickenham for practice. Geoff came up to see me in the dressing rooms.

All he said was: 'We didn't pick you because we didn't think your mobility was good enough. Here's the video we had watching you – see what you think.' And that was it. He just walked off leaving me clutching the tape. Within seconds I had just thrown it into the nearest bin. I was due to go out to train but I'd picked up some bumps and bruises the previous day and I was hardly motivated by his words. Whether Geoff ever thought very deeply about the best way to break such news to players I don't know, but I wasn't terribly impressed with the way I was treated. Even after the news that I'd been dropped I had planned to train, but when I got this brief dismissal, I was totally deflated. I felt there was no point in risking making any of the bumps and strains any worse, so I got dressed again and left.

I was very annoyed. I thought I'd played well against Canada, but even so, if Geoff had handled it in a different way I'm sure I would have reacted more positively. He could have said something like, 'Let's go and look through this video together and I'll show you what I mean. Give me your thoughts. In this particular situation we didn't think you were in the right position.' But there was none of that. He was virtually saying, 'Thanks very much, but no thanks,' and frankly, I felt aggrieved about it. I should add that I am not one to throw tantrums when things don't go my way. I accept the situation, make the best of it, and try to get on with what I have to do. But I thought this had been handled particularly poorly.

I jumped into the car and drove home to Leicester. It never crossed my mind to consider retiring from international rugby because I am not like that. Whatever else I am, I am not a quitter. I simply felt it was unjust, but when you think about it there have been many unjust decisions made over the years affecting English rugby players. I thought I'd better not stay down at Twickenham because I was so angry. The reshuffled back row was retained and I was left out of the side for the remainder of that season – I missed the whole of the 1993 Five Nations Championship, which was a bitter blow. Yet the amazing thing was that although Geoff Cooke apparently didn't think I was good enough to get into the England side throughout that Championship, I was then selected for the Lions tour to New Zealand. I can only assume that I owed my selection for the Lions to the coach, Ian McGeechan, rather than to the manager, who was of course Geoff Cooke.

Thereafter, I suppose there was always a bit of an atmosphere between Cooke and myself. I would have to admit that I never trusted him after that. It wasn't the first time he'd dropped me: I'd been left out for the quarter-final of the 1991 World Cup, against France in Paris, and was unable to regain my place in the side for the remainder of the tournament, but I could understand better why that decision had been made.

In spite of our slightly difficult relationship, I would be the first to recognize Geoff Cooke's role in turning English rugby right round in international terms. The story really began after the 1987 World Cup, when England failed so badly in the quarter-final in Brisbane against Wales. Somehow, that match seemed to represent a benchmark in England's history. Within a matter of months, Martin Green, the coach, and manager Mike Weston had gone, to be replaced by Geoff Cooke. Roger Uttley was to become the coach, but there is no doubt that Cooke was the man at the helm, making the decisions and helping to plot a path towards better times for the game in this country. I'd had to wait until 1986 for my debut for England, but I had had a taste of top-class international opposition well before that. In 1983, I had come on to the field for the Midlands against New Zealand, very late in their game at Welford Road. The Midlands had just gone ahead through a penalty and a huge dropped goal from Dusty Hare and I think there was not much more than a minute remaining. We had a scrum on our line but unfortunately Graham Robbins of Coventry had to come off at that point. He was in a hell of a state, so he probably didn't have much choice, but it was a baptism of fire for me all right – albeit a very brief one.

It had been a really hard game and I remember that Gary Rees had taken a shocking hammering. His head was cut to ribbons and his back was like Clapham Junction Station, it had so many lines running across it from the All Blacks' boots. He had played superbly, selling himself for the cause of the Midlands. So on I went, for my Midlands debut, with the game in a critical position as the Midlands fought desperately to hang on to their lead. Initially, I was disappointed not to have been picked for the match, but having seen the way the All Blacks came at the Midlands, I was quite happy to be sitting on the bench. Anyway, I packed down, we won the scrum, the ball was kicked to touch and I think there was possibly one movement after that before the final whistle blew. We had won, by 19–13.

Dusty Hare had kicked an enormous dropped goal from inside our half and everybody was so happy at the result. For an international team to beat the All Blacks is always something special; for a divisional side to do it is exceptional.

It was just over two years later that I finally won my first cap. Yet when the international season began, nothing seemed less likely. England started off with a 21–18 win over Wales at Twickenham, never a bad way to begin the Championship. But in those days it was still the old inconsistent England: occasionally good enough to lift themselves to a victory but far too often vulnerable, and unable to win on a regular basis. The second match of the tournament underlined the point, Scotland hammering us 33–6 at Murrayfield. Graham Robbins had been capped at No. 8, getting the vote ahead of me for the match with Wales. He had the considerable misfortune to play in Scotland, as well, and that proved to be his second and final England cap. I had hoped to get the call-up when Graham got in at the start of the Five Nations. We were close rivals, having battled for the No. 8 spot in the Midlands side and then England. After the defeat in Scotland, England decided they wanted to change things around for the next game, against Ireland at Twickenham.

I will never forget how the news that I was in was broken to me. I was attached to the Hinckley CID at that time and we were interviewing a group of people whom we suspected of having been involved in a lot of burglaries in the area. In the middle of the interview, someone popped his head round the door to say there was a call for me. I went outside and picked up the phone to hear Chalkie White saying, 'Well done, you're in!' I knew instantly what he meant. I was so excited about it – I think most players would tell you that the thrill of hearing of your first selection for your country is an almost unrivalled emotion for a sportsman. Certainly for this rugby player, it was.

I went back into the interview room and said to my colleague Peter Jeffery: 'I'm in.'

'What do you mean, you're in?' he said.

I explained. This chap we were interviewing must have heard part of this conversation, because he asked what it was about. I told him I played rugby for Leicester and that I'd just been chosen for England. Before that, it had been quite a difficult interview, but suddenly he blurted out: 'I feel very honoured. So I may as well tell you everything.' It was extraordinary. He came out with everything he knew and we were able to clear up a long list of burglaries!

In truth it had seemed so long ago that I'd won that first 'cap' for the Midlands that I had almost become disillusioned with my inability to break through into the international side. I felt I was ready for it, but when the selectors went for Graham ahead of me at the start of that 1986 season, it just piled on the misery for me. I hadn't done as much training as I should have done, but that week I'd told myself I had to snap out of my lethargy and get out and do some real work. So I did three or four runs that week – and then the call-up came within days!

Fran Clough, the Orrell centre, was another new cap for the match against Ireland and the night before the game the pair of us, together with Kevin Simms, Fran's fellow Cambridge University student, went to the local cinema to see *A Chorus Line*. Being a policeman, I like a decent police film or at least something with a really good storyline attached to it, but this film was about a group of dancing girls and I found it dreadfully boring. I couldn't believe I sat through the whole thing. Fran and Kevin loved it, but I thought to myself, 'Here I am, on the night before my international debut for England, bored to death. What's this all about?'

The preparations for England matches were nowhere near as thorough then. We did a bit of light training on the Thursday once we had met up, whereas now we meet on a Wednesday. But we did not have all the technical aids available to current sides – there were no videos to study, for example. You just turned up, did your own thing as a team and hoped it would be sufficient on the day. We went about it with a total disregard for what sort of side the opposition were and what they would try to do. These days, you go on to the field fully aware of almost every intricate detail of your opponents' game.

I'd joined up with an England squad which also included Rory Underwood, my team-mate at Welford Road. He had missed what had been a record defeat against Scotland in Edinburgh but was now back in the side. Much was expected of us, and of the other new men who had come into the team after the Murrayfield setback. Right wing Simon Smith, centres Jamie Salmon and Simon Halliday and prop Paul Rendall were also left out, along with Graham Robbins. John Hall was injured. The new men were Gary Rees, Gareth Chilcott, Rory Underwood, Kevin Simms, Fran Clough and me.

It was a day for which I had waited a mighty long time. I had made my international debut for the England Schools Under-19 team when I was seventeen (as a lock forward) and was then chosen for the England Under-23 squad to visit Romania. The following year I had the chance to go to Spain, too, but dislocated a shoulder and had to pull out. It was not to be the last time serious injury disrupted my career. But now, at the age of twenty-two, I was at last to make my senior debut. Local people in Leicester gave me some wonderful support. Graham Willars, then first-team coach for the Tigers, told the local paper: 'Dean has earned it. He has put in some tremendous performances. He has something very special. He has very good hands and is good on the ground as well as in the air – something they have lacked in the England side in the pack.' The Leicester local councillor, Jeremy White, even tabled a motion for the following council meeting which read: 'In view of the fact that this brings prestige of a sporting nature upon the borough, this council sends their congratulations to Dean Richards on his recent selection to the England rugby team.' I was a bit overwhelmed but delighted nonetheless to receive so many kind words from well-wishers.

And my debut went well. Rugby being a team game, it was just essential for me that England won. We did, beating Ireland 25–20, and I was fortunate enough to score two tries. I wouldn't say I was robbed of a third, but I was just about to pick up the ball and score when one of the Irish second-row boys hacked it out of my hands. The referee gave a penalty try so the team benefited. Besides, who could ask for more than two tries on a debut? I remember when I dived on the ball for the second pushover try and came up with it, Peter Winterbottom, who was winning his eighteenth cap and had been involved with England since 1982, came up to me and said: 'I've played nearly twenty bloody times for this side and not scored. You turn up and get two in your first game. There's something wrong somewhere.' But he had a grin on his face a mile wide.

It was a dream debut for me, especially as my parents were there to see it. By this time they had emigrated to Canada and were living in Montreal. They had flown over for the game, but hadn't arrived at Gatwick Airport until just four hours before kick-off time because they had had to come via New York. We did not know until late on whether the game would even be played because it was so cold and there was ice and snow around. I didn't know whether Mum and Dad had arrived safely and found their tickets, and so it wasn't until afterwards that I knew for certain that they had seen the game. That made me very pleased. It was a very happy occasion with the family around.

Someone in the press wrote afterwards that it was the best

debut by a No. 8 since Mervyn Davies's for Wales fifteen years earlier. I'm sure I wasn't in that class, but it was nice to receive the compliment. Graham Robbins, who, it was said, had kept me out of the England side earlier that season on the strength of his frequent pushover tries for the Midlands, was at Twickenham to see the game. I was more than aware that had Graham been in the side, it would have been he who would have touched down my two tries. I can only speculate as to how much longer that would have delayed my opportunity with England. Nevertheless, David Hands kindly reported in *The Times*: 'Dean Richards made his senior debut in a way which ought to bring tears of joy to England's sorely tried supporters. His intelligent reading of the game made one ache that he had not been chosen earlier.'

The fact that I scored two tries on my debut is by no means an indication that I found the higher grade of international rugby straightforward – far from it. It was a yard faster and just as physical – probably more physical than anything I had been used to. It was the greater speed that shocked me most. I felt I was off the pace. At Leicester, I knew I could make a mark on the game, take a decisive role sometimes (I'd scored sixteen tries in eight games at one stage that season) and play the game to suit myself. I found this very different. But things change and you develop, and England, we hoped, were about to start developing too. Victory gave us the prospect of an outright win in the Five Nations Championship in our final match in Paris. Yet the reality was always likely to be otherwise. In 1986, it had been four years since England had won two matches in a Five Nations Championship season, an extraordinary statistic.

Well, we went to the Parc des Princes and duly got hammered, by 29–10. I counted myself lucky just to get on to the pitch for the game. We had arrived at the Trianon Palace Hotel in Versailles, England's usual retreat whenever they go to Paris, and I was allocated a room with Maurice Colclough, our second-row forward. Maurice, dubbed the Marquis de Colclough because he'd had a spell in French rugby with

Angoulême, was a wily old bird. By this stage he had won twenty-four caps in an international career stretching back as far as 1978, and of course he'd been a member of Bill Beaumont's England Grand Slam side in 1980. He and I were given a room right up in the attic. When we got there Maurice opened the window and said, 'It's interesting here. They don't have guttering as such; it's like a walkway, a path. You can actually get along it from one room to another.'

So like a fool, the naive youngster from Leicester, about to earn his second cap, stepped out of the window and started to walk along this precarious ledge. The view when I looked over the parapet was a sight to behold. Louis the Sun King's famous palace stretched away beneath me across the square, which was all very fine – until I suddenly twigged what was going on and looked back towards the window to see the Marquis closing it behind me. I was stuck out on some dodgy roof, 100ft up in the air, and with not a thing to break my fall! I suppose I was out there for about ten minutes, nonchalantly admiring the magnificent view with trepidation in my heart, until one of the other lads let me in. When I got back, old Maurice was chuckling away to himself.

Of course, even as a new boy I should have known better, because Maurice, as everybody was aware, had been involved in one of the most sensational tricks ever pulled by a visiting player in Paris. It happened a few years before my first visit there, back in 1982, I think. Apparently, the England boys, and especially Colclough and the prop forward, Colin Smart, who was at the Welsh club Newport at the time, had been egging each other on with challenges for the whole weekend – 'Anything you can do, I can beat; any drink you can put down, I'll sink double,' that kind of thing. Maurice decided that after the match – which England had won 27–15, so they must have been in high spirits anyway – he'd slip into the dining room where the banquet was to be held and line up some practical joke on Colin. It's alleged that he saw that each player had been given a bottle of aftershave as a gift. He took his to the washroom, tipped it all out and thoroughly washed the container before refilling it with water and carefully replacing it beside his place mat. When the England players walked into the dining room an hour or so later, Maurice picked up his 'aftershave', opened the cap, said to Smart, 'Come on Smartie, see if you can do this,' and drank off the entire contents, watched by the astonished players. Smart, apparently keen to match the trick, did likewise with his bottle and was promptly taken seriously ill. He had to be rushed to a local hospital and have his stomach pumped out. So I must have been daft to believe anything Maurice told me.

When it came to the match, I was made to look even more naive. If I'd thought I was off the mark against Ireland, I was so far off it in Paris it was unbelievable. It came as a real shock to me. The game was extremely fast and the French No. 8 Jean-Luc Joinel ran rings around me. The French used to call Joinel the Sly Fox, and he was certainly too cunning for me that day. He was by no means the most physical or dirtiest of French players I have encountered, but he was a fine footballer who knew the game inside out. I think that day he was winning his forty-sixth cap.

Someone who was much more physical was Eric Champ, the back-row forward from Toulon. Eric was very aggressive but a very good player with it. The French had this move around that time whereby Champ would drop off a scrum on the left side and the ball would go to the fly-half, who would scissor with the centre. He would come up and scissor again with Champ, who took the ball on the charge. There was only one country in the world who could do that time and again and that was France. Champ took the ball extremely well on those occasions and the move created either a lot of ground or a lot of tries.

France might often play their rugby with extraordinary intensity, but once you get away from the field and the competition, most of them are really great guys. Jean-Pierre Garuet, the old Lourdes prop, played in that match in 1986, two years after his infamous sending-off in the game against Ireland in Paris. In the winter of 1991, I went skiing with my wife, Nicky, down in the Pyrenees. We flew to Lourdes and drove up into the mountains. We popped into a bar which turned out to be one owned by very good friends of Jean-Pierre, and when I next saw him, the following year at the French match, he asked me to be sure to drop in the next time I was in his area so he could entertain me.

So the 1986 season ended with England achieving a 50 per cent success rate. The following year promised to be a major one – in the summer the first-ever rugby World Cup was to be staged in Australia and New Zealand. Unfortunately for me, I was to make a terrible start to 1987.

The weather had forced a postponement of the first international of the season, against Scotland at Twickenham, in which I'd been due to play. The same team was reselected for the game against Ireland in Dublin, but in the interim I damaged the medial ligaments of my left knee in the final moments of a match against the Metropolitan Police, which took place only because the Tigers' Cup tie had been postponed due to the weather. At first, when my leg was put into plaster, it was on the cards that I might even miss the World Cup as well as the Five Nations. It was terribly frustrating, given that I had only two caps and was desperate to cement my place with some good performances that season. But I managed to get fit in time for the final international – the rescheduled match against the Scots – and we won it 21–12. That victory was to send us off to the World Cup in reasonable heart, even though we'd had a pretty poor domestic season beforehand, losing to France, Wales and Ireland.

By that time, Mike Harrison of Wakefield had taken over as the new England captain following unsavoury scenes down at Cardiff in England's 19–12 defeat by Wales. Afterwards, the RFU decided to discipline three players, skipper Richard Hill, Wade Dooley and Graham Dawe. So it was a much-changed England team that met Scotland, with Richard Harding at scrum-half, Nigel Redman at lock and Brian Moore making his debut at hooker. For my debut the previous year, Nigel Melville (Smelly to one and all) had been captain. Smelly was a good player with very quick hands, but he wasn't an inspirational captain. Mickey Harrison was different – a gentleman, a great bloke and a guy I enjoyed playing under.

Later on that year, I was invited to join a World Select XV to play the All Blacks in Japan in a one-off match. Scots like John Jeffrey and Iwan Tukalo were on that trip, together with me, Paul Rendall, Mickey Harrison and others. We got to know the Scottish boys well and enjoyed their company. It turned out to be a very boozy trip but on the actual day of the game our scratch side managed to give a very good account of itself. I seem to recall Gavin Hastings coming over very late in the trip but we also had a few Japanese players in our side. I scored a try but got a good kicking for it.

John Jeffrey and I had decided how we were going to play it in the back row. The two of us had a local Japanese guy called Hayashi at No. 6 – he later came to Oxford University and won a blue in 1990. Anyway, we managed to wind him up something rotten. We said, 'If Buck Shelford does this, you tackle him. If Buck Shelford does that, you tackle him. Whatever Buck Shelford does, you tackle him.'

We kept on at him for about ten minutes at one stage, and by the end of it he was saying over and over again to himself, 'Me tackle Buck Shelford, me tackle Buck Shelford.' He got so wound up that as he went out for the match he turned round to face a locker and headbutted it, stoving in the entire door. John and I looked at each other and wondered what we had unleashed. We almost began to feel sorry for Buck! To give him his credit, Hayashi didn't play too badly – but he didn't do any damage to Wayne Shelford.

The day after the game, which I think we lost by something like 30–9 – not too bad in the circumstances – we were all invited to go around Disneyworld in Tokyo. We'd been asked the day before the match and said we'd go. Our tickets duly arrived and off we went, together with the entire All Black squad. When we got off the coach and started to walk through the entrance, all we could hear behind us were shouts in Kiwi accents of 'Hey, these guys have tickets – where are ours?' Then they started arguing among themselves. 'I'm not paying to go in. Why the hell haven't we got tickets?' J.J. and I were highly amused. In the end, the New Zealanders stood for about three quarters of an hour outside Disneyworld, waiting for someone to go back and get them some money so they could pay to get in.

We had a very pleasant week in Tokyo. The people were terrific and most hospitable and showed us around. I've always told my wife that there are only a few places in the world I would really like to go back to and take her with me. Tokyo would be one of them.

In 1988, a tornado trading under the name of Michael Skinner won a place in the England side. Whatever our results thereafter, the humour stakes were instantly sharpened by the arrival of the Harlequins flanker. When you play for England, you get to know your fellow players pretty well and you become close. It is truly a team game, this sport, and one man standing alone is never going to be a success. You must have the mentality for working together with others for the benefit of the side. In that year's Championship, we lost narrowly in Paris to France by 10–9 (England's last Five Nations defeat against them to date) and then returned home to play Wales at Twickenham. We lost the match 11–3 to a Welsh team for which Jonathan Davies played outstandingly well on what was to be his last appearance against England before he turned professional. That fine line-out player Bob Norster also excelled himself.

When I look back on that sort of defeat, which seemed to occur all too often for England, and then reflect on where the national side now stands, I find it difficult to link the two. The modern England team has confidence in its own ability and talent and there are class players available in almost every department. In the late eighties, there simply wasn't the same confidence. Perhaps the players lacked the necessary deep belief in themselves and other nations were able to take advantage of that. It wasn't that we didn't have good players – plainly we did. But what marks out a great side from an ordinary one is often the self-belief and strong conviction that it will win. There were plenty of games during England's three Grand Slams in five years in which we might have buckled and gone under, but underpinning all those triumphs was a firm belief that we would win. It makes such a difference at that level and it is one of the major reasons for England's revival during this period.

The match against Wales in 1988 might not have been much fun, but the evening afterwards was a great deal better. Glen Webbe, the Bridgend and Wales wing, had brought a laughing box with him; he kept switching it on throughout the dinner and booms of laughter would echo around the room. It went on right through the speeches until someone grabbed hold of it and threw the thing into a bucket of cold water. It didn't have quite so much to laugh about after that.

All the back-row players from both sides were sitting at one table. Rowland Phillips, the Welsh flanker, was next to Mickey Skinner, who selected the occasion to announce himself to the world of international rugby dinners. He went off to the loo, returning just as the desserts were arriving. The hotel had created this lovely-looking pudding in the shape of a castle, a huge thing, one for each table to share. Skins took it off the waiter's tray and asked Phillips from behind if he would like some dessert. When the Welshman said yes without turning round, Skins promptly thrust the whole thing into his face. It was about 2ft by 2ft in size and made the biggest mess you've ever seen in your life. Things went from bad to worse after that. Skins and Webbe got involved in an arm-wrestling challenge match, but unfortunately for Mickey, Glen turned out to be a champion. He destroyed Skins twice, and even Mickey had had enough after that. Meanwhile, Rowland Phillips, who wasn't very happy at all, sat there very quietly for a few minutes. There was a lot of tension in the air. After a while he came round, but for a spell it looked as though things might go the wrong way completely.

Skinner's reputation is, of course, well known. He once went to a dinner in the north-east held by his old club up there, Blaydon. The club said that he could invite up to forty friends and they would foot the bill. Old mates flew in from all parts east and west, including Will Carling. Apparently there was a long table on one side of the room and most of the boys took off their jackets and draped them around the backs of their chairs. When Will made the mistake of leaving the table for a moment, someone picked up his chair, complete with jacket, and handed it to the next bloke along. He passed it on and it went down the room until it reached the last guy, who threw it out of the window from quite a height. Poor old Will had to go outside and retrieve his dirty, crumpled jacket from the flowerbed.

Rugby is a hard game and you have got to have your enjoyment. The pressure is so great at international level that you must have an opportunity to let off steam. It is, after all, only a hobby and if you are fortunate to be able to play in the national side you are putting yourself under a lot more pressure than if you were just a club player. That necessitates an escape outlet, and whether it is going out and getting drunk or throwing a gâteau in someone's face, each person reacts differently. By no means everyone goes around throwing gâteaux in people's faces, but that is Mickey Skinner's way.

Personally, I have been very lucky. I don't do very much to other people so I don't get much done back to me. I tend to organize stunts and get people to do the dirty work for me! I helped to plan a practical joke which had one of our former England squad men, the ex-Northampton hooker John Olver, sold hook, line and sinker for ages. It was in 1991, around the time of the Five Nations Championship. Olver had lined himself up for revenge because he'd been setting up everyone else for ages. I was sitting around one day discussing this with some of the guys and we agreed that we ought to try to think big, come up with the ideal sting. So we popped into Currie Motors, that big garage on the roundabout which everyone walks past on their way to and from Twickenham on match days. We saw the manager, explained our problem and asked for his co-operation. When we left, we had a couple of sheets of their headed note-paper on which we later typed up a letter and sent it off to Colin Herridge, the RFU's new media liaison man.

Colin had been well briefed and knew what to do. The letter said that as we had in our squad two of the best hookers in the Five Nations Championship, the company would like to spon-sor each of them with a car, and asked whether that would be in order. Colin went to see Brian Moore and tipped him off about what was going on. The pair of them then went and found Olver, or Owler, as he was known, and Herridge produced the letter. Mooro said, 'I'm up for it, what do you think?'

Olver almost bit off their hands in his enthusiasm. 'Yes, I want it too,' he enthused.

How Mooro kept a straight face at that stage I'll never know.

Anyway, Colin said he'd get back to Currie's about it. And, just as we had anticipated, on the next trip to Twickenham, when the team coach went past Currie's, Olver blurted out: 'I'm getting a new car from there and I'm going for a Ford Sierra Cosworth.' And every time we went past the garage over the course of the subsequent few weeks, Owler would go on about his car. He spent so much time bragging to everyone else in the team about it that he missed a few sniggers from guys who just couldn't contain themselves, because by now the whole first-team squad was in on the joke.

A little while later, another letter duly arrived, ostensibly from Currie Motors, saying that they agreed to the deal and asking for a photograph to be taken when the cars were handed over. Olver said, 'Yes, yes, no problem. I'll do it,' and rushed off to find his diary to select a suitable date. When he'd agreed a date, Mooro told him that he couldn't do that day, but suggested that John went along and picked up his car anyway. Mooro said he could easily collect his a few days later because he lived quite near the garage. Still Olver didn't smell a rat, and the suspense of it all was becoming almost impossible to bear.

We managed to get Owler all the way to Currie Motors for the handing-over ceremony before he twigged what had been going on for some weeks. It was a great wheeze, one of the best we'd ever pulled.

After the defeat by Wales, we had to go to Edinburgh to play Scotland. And what happened there was to have major repercussions for me personally, at one stage even threatening my career.

It was an infamous day in more ways than one. We won the match 9–6, but both sides received a lot of criticism afterwards for having played such a poor game. It was justified, too. The evening began in similarly dire style. My wife ripped her dress on the way out of the hotel room and I had to rush downstairs, jump into a taxi and try to find a shop still open where I could buy her another one. I found one, but by the time we had got down to the dinner, we were about half an hour late. That was the start of the trouble.

A bottle of whisky had been put on the table for the players. When I arrived, two thirds of it had already been drunk. The others said they'd drunk their share, and offered me the bottle to drink mine. I had a stab at it, even though I suspected they were having me on. John Jeffrey and Derek White were on the table, plus a few other guests. We started drinking with the meal, too, and there was a lot of food being thrown around the room. It was the worst example of rowdiness I could ever remember seeing at an international and I put it down to the fact that just about every player wanted to find some quick solace from the booze and forget all about the appalling game that afternoon.

We had stuffed tomatoes for one course and someone hurled one across the room, hitting another person on the head. The guy stood up, said, 'I'm not standing for that!' and promptly sent one flying back. Things were degenerating: it was becoming all-out war. The atmosphere between the teams on the field that day had been quite bad and this seemed a lighthearted way of dispelling the tension.

As the evening wore on, I caught up in the drinking stakes and, like almost everybody else who had played that day, started to get a bit drunk. We moved to a reception area for another drink, and as I was talking with John Jeffrey, a security guard suddenly appeared carrying the Calcutta Cup. To us in our condition it looked like a golden opportunity to do something daft. We grabbed the cup from him and ran off before he could react. If you'd asked me at that precise moment where we thought we were running to and what we were going to do with it, I couldn't possibly have told you. Anyway, we flagged down a passing car, jumped in, went down the road and around the corner and got out near a pub in Rose Street, near Princes Street. In we trooped, resplendent in our dicky bows, and walked up to the bar, clutching the famous Calcutta Cup, to ask for a couple of beers.

The guy behind the bar recognized us before he noticed the cup and said, 'Let me get you two a drink.'

'All right, then,' we said. 'Fill this.'

He filled up the Calcutta Cup with the local brew. There was a lot of beer in it by the time he'd finished, and we certainly couldn't drink it all. So we passed it on after a few minutes and it made its way down the bar, most people taking a slurp as it progressed.

Even though we were by now pretty far gone, it was clear to me when the cup came back to us that somehow it had been damaged. Reports in the papers the next day said I'd been kicking it down Princes Street trying to drop a goal with the thing, but I can't recollect any of that. I would be mortified to think I had done anything like that, and I honestly have no memory of such an act. Admittedly, I was drunk at the time, but I wouldn't say I was so drunk that I wouldn't have been able to remember what I'd done that night. Anyway, when we realized that the cup had been damaged we thought we'd better take it back. But first, having looked at it to see what was wrong, I thought I might try knocking the dent out myself, so I found a piece of wood and started trying to lever it back into shape. It didn't work and I abandoned the idea.

We crept back to the hotel fearing the worst, of course. I saw a porter and just said, 'Can you pop this under Don Rutherford's door, please?' I don't know whether the porter took it up to the RFU technical director or not but I do know that at 7 a.m. Roger Uttley, our coach, was banging on my door asking what the hell I had done.

Of course, because the cup was in my possession when it was damaged I had to take full responsibility for it. A hell of a fall-out ensued. The repair bill came to a thousand pounds and I immediately offered to pay it out of my own pocket. That proved unnecessary as it was covered by the insurance, but needless to say, both the RFU and the SRU were furious.

I was carpeted by the RFU within ten days. They told me they were very disappointed in me. They had thought I was a responsible young man and could not understand what I had done and why. But perhaps the fact that I offered to pay for the repair of the cup slightly eased their dismay. Geoff Cooke, the England team manager, was there and to give him his due he stood by me. He explained to the committee how the evening had gone, although most of them would have known that already because they were there too. I received a one-match international ban, which prevented me from playing against Ireland in the Dublin Millennium celebration match, while John Jeffrey was banned for six months, which meant he missed the World Sevens tournament in Australia. In some respects we both suffered, but I was not punished as severely as J.J.

It has been said many times since that the Scottish Rugby Union have never forgiven the RFU for what they regarded as the RFU's leniency towards me over that incident. Certainly, the Scots committee was aggrieved that I wasn't given a longer suspension, but that wasn't up to me. I didn't decide the sentence, and to be fair I thought it was lenient myself. I certainly expected a stiffer punishment.

But the trouble did not end there for me. I had to go before
my chief constable and explain why a young police officer had
behaved so badly in a public place. He was right to castigate
me and his lecture about expecting rather better conduct from
a policeman was completely justified. It was made pretty clear
to me that any recurrence of such behaviour would have very
severe consequences for my career. In all probability, I would
be looking for another job. The police were clearly not amused
at what had gone on and, when I had sobered up, neither
was I.

It is possible that the wild excesses of the night might not
have occurred had women been allowed into the dinner with
the players. I hadn't seen Nicky all evening because she was
with the wives and girlfriends at their own dinner, which is the
custom in rugby circles in this part of the world. But I prefer
separate after-match dinners. It is nice for the players to be able
to sit down and mingle and talk about the game, rather than
having to look after their wives and girlfriends. This view might
not go down too well with the women's rights brigade, but
there is nothing better than having a chat about the game afterwards with your opponents or colleagues and enjoying a good
laugh. If the women join us it inhibits the evening. Besides, a
lot of the wives and girlfriends prefer separate dinners themselves. They can see the rugby men want to discuss the match
on their own, and they may well want to talk about something
else.

Looking back now, the incident with the Calcutta Cup
remains something I bitterly regret. I let myself and my country
down and I will always have cause to reproach myself for that.
With something as prestigious as the Calcutta Cup, which has
so much history attached to it, you feel more than disappointed
to be responsible for damaging it. I am also sorry that the Scots
still feel quite bitter about it. I just hope that as new players
and officials come on to the scene, the memories will start
to fade.

We had one more match to play in the Championship that

season and a remarkable affair it was, too. We trailed Ireland
3–0 at half-time at Twickenham but finished winners by 35–
3. We hadn't scored a try all season but now ran them in as if
they were two a penny. We lost Nigel Melville, who sadly suffered so serious a leg injury that he never played international
rugby again. When he went off, John Orwin, the lock forward
from Bedford, assumed the captaincy. And what a leader he
turned out to be! To give him his due, John played pretty well
in the four international matches that season, but when we went
on tour that summer to Australia, he just didn't pull his weight
at all. I think it went to his head, really, and he became probably
the worst England captain I've ever known. In Australia he
seemed to think that he could have and do anything he wanted
simply because he was the England captain. He rubbed everybody up the wrong way; no one could relate to him at all. John
missed an awful lot of training sessions, saying he'd got injuries.
He did have some, but sometimes you have to play through
them. He wasn't doing that, and the players felt very let down
by him. It is vital that the captain is respected by the players –
you can't go into a game with someone you don't respect as
your leader. I think Geoff Cooke was aware of this towards the
end of the Australian tour, but in the meantime we lost the two
Tests to the Wallabies, 22–16 in Brisbane and 28–8 in Sydney,
and I think it became pretty obvious that England needed a new
captain.

All sorts of names were bandied about as candidates, mine
included. But there was never a chance of me taking on the
captaincy. Even if they had asked me, I would have turned it
down. I was too young and I didn't have an interest in leadership
at that time. I just wanted to play and get on with my game.
And the guy they picked was clearly the right man for the job,
as he has since proved. The fiasco over his sacking by the RFU
committee just before the World Cup served only to emphasize
that. The media have had an increasing influence in rugby matters over the past few years, and Will Carling has done a superb
job in handling them. He has kept the press off the players'

backs, although in doing so it may have made him look as though he was promoting himself. If that is true, then I have no worries at all about it. In many ways, I think the fact that he has been in the limelight has increased the popularity of rugby players all over the country. We are all worth far more in the eyes and minds of the media now than we have ever been before, and much of that is down to Will.

So English rugby was on the verge of change. True, the Aussies had dumped us twice Down Under, but despite the results, there was room for some optimism. A better, stronger, more cohesive pack was slowly emerging as players like Brian Moore, Wade Dooley, Gareth Chilcott, Jeff Probyn and Mickey Skinner made their presence felt. It all began from there. Later the same year, when the Australians returned to England and we beat them 28–19 in the Test at Twickenham, a young nipper by the name of Paul Ackford made his debut and was an immediate success. At the age of thirty-one he might not exactly have formed the cornerstone of England's new youth policy, but Ackers was a fine forward who added enormously to the growing quality of that pack. Ackers could and should have been on that stage earlier. He was probably overlooked because he spent so much time with lesser-known clubs like Plymouth Albion, Rosslyn Park and Metropolitan Police. Had he joined Harlequins sooner, he would almost certainly have been picked before then.

We were starting to build a team which could prove its potential as a unit for the future. What it needed was a man in charge who would give it time to develop and find the necessary cohesion. Geoff Cooke was that man. Before he arrived, it always seemed as if internationals were just one-off games. There was no obvious long-term strategy or plan. If you won, then fine, the chances were that the side would be kept intact. If England lost, then all manner of changes could be expected, which was, of course, no recipe whatsoever for lasting success.

Cooke's great contribution was his awareness that continuity and faith in team selection were badly needed. It might have been the players who initially made the England side, but it was Cooke as manager who made sure everything ran like clockwork. England's habit of picking people and then dropping them for the next game had become a bad joke. We got through players like there was no tomorrow. Geoff ensured that if you did the business, by and large you stayed on the scene. I suppose I was an exception at times, but compared to earlier years, from the sixties, seventies right through to the early eighties, there was nothing like as much chopping and changing of sides and stability in selection was achieved.

Another factor in the improving fortunes of English rugby was the introduction of the Leagues. It helped players like Paul Ackford to identify a target level on which to try to operate, and once they were there, they were much better prepared for international rugby. Geoff Cooke was the right man at the right time as far as England were concerned. Some say that he was fortunate to have been in charge of the national side at a time when there were so many good players available, which was partly true. But remember that England have always had some fine players, even in teams which were whitewashed in the Championship. It was just that no one got the best out of them. Behind the playing front you always have to have the back-room boys, and to make everything work smoothly, those guys have to be doing their jobs effectively.

Geoff did have his shortcomings, principally when it came to the game itself. Normally, though, he left that side of things up to Roger Uttley or the senior players, who knew basically the sort of game plan we would adopt.

When I first got into the England side, no one really had a clue where they were or for how much longer they were going to be around, the captain included. But from late 1988 onwards, after we beat Australia, very much the same group of players was used right through to the 1991 World Cup. And when people are together as long as that, you get to know each other very well. You might think that resentment could have arisen because certain players seemed immune from being dropped, but that wasn't how we in the squad saw it. None of us ever felt that we were completely safe from dismissal; we always knew that we had to perform to retain our places. But there is a difference between that and being afraid of making a single mistake in case you are dropped for it, which was the case in the early 1980s. All that changed under Cooke's management, and that was a major reason why so many players began to produce their top form.

England did not win every match or every honour which was available to them under Geoff Cooke. And questions were rightly asked about such defeats as the one in Edinburgh for the 1990 Grand Slam showdown and Cardiff in 1989. We came very close to winning the Championship, losing by only 12–9 to Wales in 1989 and 13–7 to Scotland the following year. And I'm sure I am not alone in thinking that England should have added the Championship in those two seasons to their list of other recent successes.

In 1989 we went down to Cardiff having beaten France 11–0 in one of the hardest international matches I can remember. Unfortunately, the weather in Wales that day played right into the hands of the host nation. Robert Norster won the line-outs for them and Robert Jones gave a masterful performance in raising up-and-unders behind our defence. It was desperately difficult to play creative rugby in such conditions and we just lost out. We just did not get our preparation for the game right on that occasion. We went out expecting it to be dry and we stuck to our original dry-weather game plan. We shouldn't have done that. We should have changed our approach as soon as we saw the bad weather. Ultimately, I suppose, it was down to the coach and captain, but with a squad as experienced as we were, there should have been enough people to make the point that a change in tactics was needed. I include myself in this. It was mentioned on the Friday because the forwards were particularly concerned that we were not preparing for both types of game. It was quite sunny that day but when it came to match day, it was chucking it down with rain. The forwards mentioned their doubts to the backs, but were told that everything would be all right. Norster, Jones and their colleagues saw to it that it wasn't, of course, but we learned a lot from that experience.

I missed the whole of the 1990 season with a damaged shoulder, including the tour to Argentina, although I did get my place back when Argentina visited Twickenham later that year for the autumn international. I had first had trouble with it against France back in 1989. I went down on my shoulder in that match and it was quite sore afterwards. Then I went on the Lions tour of Australia later that year and did it again a couple of times over there. It was so bad by the end that I couldn't play in the final match against the Anzacs. When I was tackling or stretching out it just seemed to either come out of place or give me great pain. I found out that what was happening was that it was partially dislocating and then going straight back in again. Had it been a total dislocation, the medical guys would have known exactly what the trouble was, but as it was the problem took a while to diagnose. Eventually I had a scan, which showed quite a bit of cartilage and soft-tissue damage, and I had to have an operation. Unfortunately, during the stitching up, one of the nerves got trapped in my shoulder and they had to open it up again to release it. But the operation itself was a success, so although I had to miss that season I was able to concentrate on looking ahead to 1990–1.

Being away from the scene when England went to Murrayfield for the Grand Slam showdown with Scotland that March was not the nicest experience I've ever known in my rugby life. I was on police duty that day, working on crowd control at Filbert Street, the home of Leicester City FC. I took my Walkman along with me so that I could be right up with the news as soon as I had a chance to listen in. Unfortunately, because of the noise coming off the terraces at Filbert Street, I couldn't hear a thing. Afterwards, I was walking around asking complete strangers whether they'd heard the score. 'Two–one,' was all they said, of course. In fact, I didn't get the result until

I got back to Hinckley Police Station and someone told me. I was very disappointed for the lads and surprised, too, because I felt that we were a far better side than the Scots.

Nevertheless, I did not share what I saw as the over-confidence of some members of the England squad. On the morning of the game, I'd been on my way out of the house when the telephone had rung. It was Mike Teague calling from the England team hotel. He said, 'Hey, big man, you're talking to a Five Nations Grand Slam winner here.'

'What on earth do you mean?' I asked.

'Well, we're going to win today,' he told me.

'Not with that attitude, you're not,' I replied.

We had a bit of a chat and I wished him all the best, but I would say that it gave an indication of the attitude of the players on the day. I think everybody thought it was going to be easy. England had played some very good rugby during the course of that season, but you should never ever underestimate the Scots anywhere – and certainly not at Murrayfield.

I didn't want to watch the game afterwards and to this day I have never seen the whole match, just the occasional excerpt. Watching rugby matches in which I am not involved is not my idea of fun.

The scars of that particular day were to last a long time in the England camp. They were not totally erased even by the achievement of the Grand Slam the following season, or by the one after that. But perhaps what happened at Murrayfield that day was another learning phase the England team needed to go through. It made us hungrier, more determined; there was no resting on laurels, as two successive Grand Slams afterwards confirmed.

By then, too, England had become a solid, efficient and tal-ented outfit with quality players in the team and others waiting to take their places in the event of injuries or loss of form. The long years of constant changes within the side had become a distant memory and England were working to a proper plan and policy. The national side under Geoff Cooke had gone from something of a joke team which rarely sustained a successful challenge to one that won Grand Slams, Triple Crowns, Calcutta Cups and played in a World Cup final. The transformation was considerable.

6 A Trio of Grand Slams

For me, the 1991 Grand Slam was the one that almost never happened. I had come desperately close to turning my back on the entire England set-up. I'd had a year out, which had included the 1990 Grand Slam defeat by Scotland at Murrayfield, when I was invited back to a training session at Newcastle Gosforth, which tied in with the opening of their new clubhouse. When we went out for the session, I was amazed to discover that the person taking the forwards' session because Roger Uttley couldn't get there that day was Don Rutherford, the RFU's technical director.

I just stood there in disbelief at how the session developed. I'd never seen anything like it. Here, in 1991, was a man who had represented England as long ago as the mid-1960s, trying to organize a coaching session almost thirty years later. It was just so old-fashioned in its style. To say the game had changed in that time would be the understatement of the year, but somehow Rutherford had got the job on the day. What was more, the bloke who was telling us forwards the ins and outs of line-outs, scrummaging, rucking and mauling, had been a back. Everybody just stood there wondering what was going on. What we were being asked to do was so incredible that I remember thinking, 'What have I come back for? I think I've made the wrong decision. I don't want to be back here if this is what it's like.'

Quite honestly, I'd enjoyed my year away from it all. I'd been able to go out eating and drinking with my friends without even thinking about my weight. A look at my physique probably told the story – I had blossomed to 19½ stone! But I had done some pre-season training so I wasn't in too bad a shape when I arrived for the England get-together.

When I came back, some people thought I had a point to prove to Geoff Cooke, who had left me out of the Grand Slam decider in Scotland. But I didn't feel as though I had a thing to prove to Cooke – I just wanted to prove a point to myself, that was all. I felt I still wanted to achieve something in rugby life in England. I'd been on a victorious British Lions tour to Australia but had yet to win a Triple Crown, Grand Slam or anything like that.

Mind you, the season had already had its pitfalls. When the Midlands played the North in a divisional match at Otley in December, I took Nicky up there for the weekend. The idea was that we would spend the Sunday walking out on the Yorkshire moors. But halfway through the game, Dewi Morris welcomed me regally by taking me out with a sliding tackle which badly sprained my ankle and put me out of rugby for five weeks. Everything had gone wrong that weekend – it snowed heavily and by the time we got through the worst of the weather to reach our hotel, my ankle was badly swollen and I was hobbling around hopelessly. The walking next day was impossible and I had to sit around like the lord of the manor, supping Yorkshire ales and waiting for Nicky to drive me home at the end of the day.

By the time we got to January, we had already prepared hard for the opening match of the Championship, against Wales in Cardiff. We'd beaten them at Twickenham the year before and saw no reason why we shouldn't do so again – except that England hadn't won in Cardiff for twenty-eight years and the old bogey refused to lie down. The papers were full of it, saying we weren't up to the task and writing us off continually. The stick they gave us before the match had even kicked off was appalling and it was to have dire consequences for them afterwards.

From the time we met up that week almost to the point when

we drove to the ground, Geoff Cooke had 'Land of My Fathers' playing at us from the stereo machine. At team meetings, we were bombarded with videos of great Welsh games with the singing roaring out. But all of a sudden, on the last night before the game, he said, 'You've been hearing the Welsh singing and watching them score tries and win games. Now here's how well *we* can play.' And he ran a video compilation of extracts from England's defeat of Wales the previous year, concentrating on all the best parts from England's point of view. It was the ideal mental approach for us. Perhaps on the day we didn't play particularly well, but Simon Hodgkinson's kicking, which punished Welsh mistakes and infringements, plus Mike Teague's try from a wheeled scrum did the job. It wasn't entertaining rugby, but it was a game we just had to win the best way we could to break the sequence. And we did – by 25–6.

It was my first Five Nations match since 1989, a long, long break. But I could see the potential of the England side, just as I'd seen it in 1989, when we should have won the Championship. Only a defeat in Cardiff, for which we were largely to blame, lost us the title that year.

After the match came the fuss with the press when the England management and captain refused to speak to them. But it wasn't only them: because of all the stick we'd been given and the bad things that had been written, we said in the dressing room that if anyone didn't want to speak to them, then they shouldn't. Deep down, the players were as one in feeling aggrieved about it. We'd always been available for them over the years, and for them to turn on us for no reason before we'd even played the game was over the top. We felt that perhaps they needed to be taught a lesson, namely that you have to give a little and take a little in life.

Will Carling was criticized for this stance later, unjustly, in my view. It was a classic case of a missed opportunity for the RFU to develop closer links with the players and help to establish a stronger bond between us. I thought they should have taken a lead and said to the press that they could hardly expect co-operation from the players if they were going to write such bilge.

What happened happened, and would have done no matter who was manager or captain of the England side. Geoff Cooke and Will Carling did not arrange it themselves; it was a shared view in the camp. Perhaps what led to it all symbolized the changes that were taking place in the game.

These days, so many more people are interested in rugby that it is no longer just the true rugby reporters who cover it. Now you have press men who are interested only in looking for stories, usually of a personal nature. They want these stories not to benefit rugby football, but to sell newspapers. I think this has damaged the relationship between the true rugby writer and the player. You used to feel that you could chat to all the rugby journalists around because generally they were all the same – very strong supporters of the game. But now you are never quite sure who your friends are. The times when you were able to have a good chat and a beer or two with the press lads and know that what you said privately would not be reported seem to have gone. I am not pleased that non-rugby journalists, often people who have covered soccer throughout their careers but now suddenly profess to be world experts on Rugby Union, are reporting on the game. In my view, they are giving people the wrong perspective.

Anyway, after the match in Cardiff, we returned to Twickenham and beat Scotland 21–12, which meant a lot to the boys who had lost up there the previous year. It wasn't that big a deal to me because all the times I had played against them, I'd ended up on the winning side. I knew that with the Scots you had to play the game up front, at your pace and not in the frenetic way which they like because it disrupts you. Providing that we kept to that tight, controlled game I couldn't see them troubling us, and so it proved. Incidentally, few people may know this, but I might easily have been out there that day wearing the blue shirt of Scotland. My mother was born in Scotland and both her parents came from there, too. Mind you, their parents were born in Lithuania, so I suppose I might have ended up playing for them. Now that would have been interesting!

In between the two internationals, there had been another example of the regimentation which had begun to creep into the England set-up. Nicky and I went skiing over in France and when we got back, I bumped into Geoff Cooke at the next get-together. He asked me where I'd been because he had been trying to get hold of me. I saw no reason to tell him anything but the truth. He said, 'Oh, oh, I see. Do you not consider that to have been a little dangerous?'

I replied that it might have been, but nothing had happened and you could construe going out for a walk in winter as dangerous because you might slip over on the ice and hurt yourself. Personally, I thought it was good training. I probably got fitter over there than I would have done if I had stayed in England. But it was clear that Geoff didn't see it that way.

'And if you had broken your leg?' he asked me.

'Then I would have broken it. Too bad,' I replied. 'It's like getting run over or crashing your car – if it's going to happen, it's going to happen.'

If you want to call this mainly an amateur sport, then players have got to be able to do their own thing. The authorities can't have it both ways. Players must have the right to choose where they want to go and when, and to do whatever they wish. I am sure that the powers that be would like us to be wrapped up in cotton wool and just brought out for the internationals. But they have not been prepared to follow that line of argument to its logical conclusion by agreeing to allow players financial benefit. They want the best of both worlds, a view which has led to so much difficulty over the future course of the sport. If rugby is amateur, as the RFU have insisted it is, they should not have presided over a set-up which frowned on players going off and doing what they liked. If skiing takes your fancy, then you should be able to go – that is the advantage of an amateur sport. A professional sport would not allow you to do that sort of thing, which is why so much in the game will change if it does become professional.

With me unscathed from my skiing trip, we went to Ireland and, after some alarms, clinched the Triple Crown. It was a game we eventually won 16–7, but the wet conditions gave us problems. Even so, I think some of our difficulties were caused by our own sub-standard attitude on the day. The forwards had been keyed up for it all right, because we knew it was going to be tough. But on the morning of the match in our hotel, we were greeted with the ridiculous sight of the backs running around the hotel having talcum-powder fights and playing silly games. Then they saw all the forwards staring at them with an expression that said if they made one more move, we would kill them. That stopped them. We virtually told them to grow up. So we were not sufficiently mentally prepared for the game, yet somehow we snatched a win. Perhaps the team over-extended Thursday night's light approach of visiting a pub just up the road from the hotel. They're great in there; very hospitable and friendly. They all try to buy us a pint and get us drunk, and it's become a regular trip when we play over there.

Rory Underwood's try was crucial. The ball got shovelled back from the forwards but it was slow ball. Rob got caught with it, and he passed it on to Jerry, who gave it to me. I remember going to the floor and setting it up and Jeff Probyn coming in and going to pick it up. I yelled at him to leave it, the ball went out and down the line to Rory, and he scored in the corner. Later on, Mike Teague scored in the opposite corner.

The win set up another Grand Slam showdown, a winner-take-all match to round off the season, because the French too had won their first three matches. But this time they were to meet us at Twickenham, and although we conceded one of the greatest tries ever scored in international rugby, a 100-yard move started by Serge Blanco from behind the French posts and touched down under our posts by Philippe Saint-André, I always felt we had the game under control. We hadn't lost to them since 1988, and we knew that if we played as a team, we had a pretty good chance of beating them again. And so we did – by 21–19 – even though a couple of late scores from France made it closer on the scoreboard than it had seemed in the match itself.

The feeling of having achieved the Grand Slam was wonderful. We felt we had won something worth winning because most of the sides we had played were very good. The French, for example, had some great players – Blanco, Sella, Saint-André, Camberabero, Berbizier, Ondarts, Benazzi. It wasn't the same the following year because I don't think the teams we played against were that great.

The 1992 Grand Slam began in Scotland, but I was back on the bench. This, remember, was just a couple of months after the World Cup, and I was still out of favour. The old lack of mobility, I suppose. They thought I was on my last legs and as Mike Teague was to miss the entire Five Nations season through injury, they chose Tim Rodber alongside Mickey Skinner and Peter Winterbottom. I was extremely disappointed but not at all surprised. I realized that after the World Cup, the latter stages of which I'd missed out on, they were looking at my speed around the park and if anything was going to let me down in selection, that was what it would be.

As far as I was concerned, when I was out there, I was no liability to anyone. I thought I was effective and could offer England what every back row needs: balance. You can't have three flyers in a back row or three people doing the same thing. You need players who complement each other, and I felt I could provide something not many others could: a footballing brain which gave me the ability to read a game and do the right things at the right time in the right places, and in a way, to direct others, too. That role is not obvious, because nobody sees me on the field yelling my head off at players. It's not necessary to shout and gesticulate. Why do you need to shout if it's possible to speak to them calmly? At times I get angry enough to raise my voice but I am very quick to apologize, because that is not usually the way to get the best out of people. Encouragement is what works for a lot of players.

So there we were at Murrayfield and it turned out that I was required after all. This came as a shock to me, and perhaps put a question-mark over my activities on the day before the match. On the Friday, after a light training run, I had gone out shooting with John Olver. We had a good day and decided to pop into a little local we came across in the countryside outside Edinburgh. One thing led to another, and we ended up having four or five pints. On the day before a match that was not the best thing in the world to do, but then we were both reserves and if you look at the records, how many times are reserves required in internationals? Very rarely indeed.

Of course, we were by no means drunk or anything like that, but I will admit that we were sucking mints like they were going out of fashion all the way back to the hotel. When we got there we got the key to Peter Winterbottom's room and popped up there while he was downstairs, leaving a pigeon we had shot in his toilet. When he went up to his room that night after our team meeting, he went into the bathroom. Olver and I had followed him up there, at a safe distance, and when the loo was flushed, a roar of 'Olver!' came hurtling down the corridor. We took one look at each other and bolted.

About an hour into the match the next day, Tim Rodber was injured and it immediately became clear that I was needed to go on. That was all very well, except that Dick Best, who was by then coach in succession to Roger Uttley, and I got stuck in the lift trying to get downstairs on to the pitch at the stadium. We had to prise open the lift doors and Bestie was going bananas. In reality it didn't take us long to get out but it seemed like an eternity. I joined a game that had been very loose and helped to tighten it up. I know people gave me a lot of credit for coming on and playing the right game, but I felt that England were getting on top anyway at that point. All I did was rein things in a bit, which the Scots didn't want to see us do at all.

The only problem was that near the end I began to flag.

I wondered why, because I thought I'd been fit, and then I remembered the few pints I'd had the day before. That probably didn't help, but when you are flagging you look for a reason. I would be the first to say that perhaps it wasn't the most professional thing I have ever done in my career. But the way I look at it is like this. I just like to enjoy myself, and if I didn't enjoy myself, I wouldn't play rugby any more. And if playing rugby meant giving up things like going for a drink, then perhaps I would give up rugby. If a coach told me I couldn't do this or I couldn't do that, I would ignore it and carry on. If the management said, 'Right, you are dropped because of this,' then I would tell them where to stick it. Apart from feeling a bit tired late in that Scottish match, I can honestly say that my performances for England have never been impaired by my having gone skiing, had a few pints or generally done my own thing.

Rugby now tends to take over your life too much, and with the intensity with which you play today, the enjoyment factor diminishes, so much so that you have to go out and look for it. So when I'm involved in rugby, and if I have the time, I like to do some things I also enjoy, such as going shooting or popping into the pub for a couple of pints with my friends.

Different people have different ways of preparing for a game, so you cannot expect everyone to behave in the same way. Some like to sit and watch videos, others prefer to lock themselves away in their room. I am a bit more relaxed than that. I think I have the ability to switch on ten minutes or so before a game or just as the whistle goes.

After we beat Scotland, I was back on the bench again when Ireland visited Twickenham. I'd thought I had a good chance of holding the place I had taken at Murrayfield when Tim was injured, not at the expense of Tim, but of Mickey Skinner, because I had been very disappointed with the way he'd played. Mickey had an extraordinary habit of being able to put in very big tackles but in a limited area. That Scotland game, I felt, exposed him more than any other match I'd seen him play. His game was all about big hits and big rushes. Tim offered rather more craft in the back row and around the field his handling was a lot better. He read a game more than Mickey, too. I thought they would leave Mickey out, move Tim to No. 6 and keep me at No. 8. It was not to be. But we beat Ireland 38–9 and Mickey Skinner played a lot better in that game. Tim Rodber, too, kept up his form, or so I thought. However, when the side to go to Paris was announced, Tim was omitted and I was recalled, which I thought was tough on Tim. I would have kept him at No. 6 and put Mickey on the bench, because it was time for England to look to the future.

The match was dubbed 'Le Crunch' and it certainly turned out that way. France had two players sent off, Lascubé and Moscato, and it would have been quite justifiable had another couple of them gone. Tordo was very lucky to stay on the field and the forward who rushed into a maul and kneed Will Carling in the head at full pace should never have played again. How he didn't take Will's head off I will never know. But the French can be like that, and in some ways it was the most unpleasant French side I have ever played against. I watched the video carefully afterwards and some of the things Tordo and the props were doing were ludicrous and dangerous. They showed no control whatsoever in their play, they just went out to try to intimidate us. Some people accused us of winding them up, and it's true that when they began to punch and kick us, old soldiers like Jeff Probyn, Brian Moore and I just laughed at them, and that got them even more incensed. They wound themselves up – we weren't responsible. They tried to play a very physical game with a lot of cheap shots. When they realized that we were disciplined and could take it and ignore them, they got frustrated.

Sometimes the French do hurt you, but what is a bruise or a gash on the head? It will have healed after five or ten days. Indiscipline has often been the French *bête noire*, yet in 1995 in our match against them at Twickenham, we had probably one of the cleanest international matches I have ever known, so they can play controlled rugby when they want to.

Reaching in front of Wayne Shelford to win the ball. We beat
Northampton 28–6 and went on to defeat Harlequins in the final
of the 1993 Pilkington Cup. *(Allsport)*

One of my favourite annual matches: the post-Christmas encounter with the Barbarians. Here I am showing the Scottish fly-half Craig Chalmers a clean pair of heels. A normal, everyday occurrence, of course...*(Allsport)*

The match that effectively decided the 1994–5 Courage League First Division Championship. We beat Bath at Welford Road to take a decisive advantage over them in the title race. *(Allsport)*

At last I get my hands on the Courage League trophy as the proud captain of Leicester Tigers. *(Allsport)*

On tour with the 1993 Lions in New Zealand. A fishing trip up the Bay
of Islands. *(Ross Kinnaird)*

OPPOSITE:
Showing the flag Down Under. *From left to right*: Rory Underwood,
me, Rob Andrew, Ieuan Evans and Brian Moore, celebrating the 1989
British Lions victory over Australia. *(Allsport)*

Battered, bruised and bloodied maybe, but it was the Australians who were finally beaten in the 1995 World Cup quarter-final. *(Allsport)*

OPPOSITE:
The efforts of Will Carling, Victor Ubogu and Tim Rodber in crunching an Australian victim epitomize our level of commitment in the quarter-final. *(Allsport)*

OVERLEAF:
England line up to face another 'Haka' in the 1995 World Cup semi-final. I felt our preparation for the match had not been good enough. *(Allsport)*

We won that 1992 match 31–13 and came home to defeat Wales comfortably, by 24–0, at Twickenham to win a second successive Grand Slam. But it felt a little flat compared to the previous year. We had not been very stretched in achieving it and the opposition was nothing to write home about. And the truth was, we had still under-achieved as a side even if we were trumpeted as winners of the first back-to-back Grand Slam since the 1920s. We didn't win as well as we would have liked. The French game was our best performance, but the Welsh match wasn't anything special.

For me, it had been a strange in-and-out season. But I didn't resent this because when I did get into the side, I always made sure I enjoyed myself and did my own thing. If you can continue to interest yourself there is no reason why you should get too disheartened. As I have always said, it is only a game. The only disappointing thing about it all is that I was often sitting on a bench all afternoon when I could have been playing rugby somewhere else. I'd have much rather done that. It is true that when you are a reserve you still have a considerable input and are among friends, enjoying the company of people with whom you get on with. The real shame was that I was away from my wife so much of the time.

I had the feeling that I was left out for certain matches because I didn't fit the model Geoff Cooke wanted and I made it clear I would not change. I remember in 1993, when I came back from the Lions tour, somebody came up to me – John Elliott, the assistant manager, I think it was – and said he'd been told that Dean Richards was a new man, he actually trained now. He was obviously unaware that I did actually train before. I think he thought I just went out shooting and drinking. I do put a little bit in just to get my fitness levels up!

I don't know if I'd go so far as to say that I have enjoyed cultivating this image and setting my stall out to tweak the tail of officialdom, but I certainly haven't minded doing so. It may have cost me a few caps, but it is more important that I've remained my own man. If some of the boys there now can honestly say they have always enjoyed sitting around for hours watching rugby videos, then their idea of fun is very different from mine. I prefer a game of three-card brag. If I've got time after that to study a video for four or five hours, which some of the boys do, then fair enough, but I won't make it my priority.

Perhaps I would have had a greater empathy with the guys who played for England in the 1970s, when it was all so much less structured and precise, although I don't think I'd have been able to compete with them in the drinking stakes in those days!

It has all got a little too serious these days. Consequently, when you do go off skiing or shooting, you find yourself doing so almost in secret rather than being open about it. You don't want too many people to know about, say, a Friday afternoon shooting trip, and that takes the gloss off some of it. If you've had a good day you like to talk to people about it. I don't see any good reason why you should have to keep it under your hat.

I think the influence of coaching in the game has become too overpowering, but that can only happen if you let it. If you are prepared to allow people to dominate you then you must expect it. You've got to stand up for yourself, especially in rugby; you've got to be prepared to say 'Stop it,' if you are training too much and are no longer having a good time. My advice is, if you feel you are not getting out of rugby what you should be, slow down and find the time to do something enjoyable. Some of the guys these days are so wound up about success in rugby that they don't see anything else.

One thing of which I am sure is that I don't regret my approach to it; not at all.

At the start of our 1995 Five Nations campaign I began to keep a diary, jotting down our schedule and my thoughts at the time. I hope what follows will provide some insight into what goes on in between the games as well as during them throughout the three months of the Championship. It certainly isn't all glamour, by any means . . .

Saturday 14 January 1995

It's cold, it's wet and the weather forecast for next Saturday, when England start the Five Nations Championship season against Ireland in Dublin, is not good. Meanwhile, Orrell came to Leicester, traditionally a tough, close match with little given away by either side. We won 29–19 but I couldn't play because I had flu. Even so, I still had to go down to Richmond to the England team hotel to prepare with the boys for next week's international, but as soon as I arrived I was sent straight off to bed so as not to contaminate any of the squad. I suppose some would say I shouldn't have gone at all, but I might improve a lot during the night and be able to train tomorrow.

Sunday 15 January

Of course, that didn't happen. I woke up feeling even worse after the exertions of the long drive down to Surrey from the midlands. There wasn't much point in hanging around feeling miserable, so I got back into the car and drove home. I couldn't go back to bed, though. I was on police duty starting at 2 p.m., and because I will be off for the latter half of the week anyway I wanted to make up some of the time. I felt I should go to work even though I wasn't feeling 100 per cent.

Wednesday 18 January

Worked from 6 a.m. to midday, then drove straight off to Richmond for an afternoon training session. Thank goodness I was better from the flu, but when I got to Richmond, only a couple of the other lads were there. Far from everyone being ready to start training at 2 p.m. as agreed, it transpired that most of the squad were still at a Cellnet lunch. They didn't arrive until 2.30. Obviously we are preparing for a big game, and in my view, having to be at a lunch which dragged on took people's minds off the reason we were there in the first place. This sort of thing has only really started to happen this season, and as far as Playervision, the players' company, is concerned, it is necessary. But at the same time it is all a bit of a distraction. If training sessions are scheduled to start at 2 p.m., it should mean 2 p.m. and we should stick to that time. I wasn't the only one standing around out on the pitch waiting for others to arrive. It is not ideal preparation and, as it turned out, it wasn't an ideal session anyway. I still felt tired and breathless due to the flu.

Our 7 p.m. meeting was very tense because everybody was aware of the task facing us. During dinner, we wound up Brian Moore mercilessly about the Irish hooker, Keith Wood, who has been receiving lots of publicity and has been described as one of the best hookers in the world. We left newspapers with big features on Wood where we were sure Brian would see them. All the rave media reviews for Wood have got Brian more and more incensed.

I had an early night, but as I was rooming with Victor 'Mr Telephone' Ubogu, I didn't get much sleep. He spends most of his free time on his mobile phone. God knows what his bills must be like.

Thursday 19 January

Team meeting at 9.30 a.m. We have a lot of these sessions and use them to go through things like details of back-row moves, what our different options are, the call signs for line-outs and scrums, that sort of thing. They are really designed to enable us to look at what is ahead and rehearse our moves, and they keep everybody sharply focused. When I first became part of the England squad we had about two team meetings before an international, but these days it's more like twenty-two. They can get boring, but some good always comes out of them. And if you bring away only one point to remember from such a meeting it has been worthwhile. The quiet people, players like Leonard and Johnson, usually sit at the back and say nothing. Then you've got those who do a lot of talking – Will Carling,

Rob Andrew and Mooro. I occasionally chip in and so does Tim Rodber. Jack Rowell is there all the time and normally leads the meeting with Will.

Next we trained at the Bank of England ground, which was unusually hard in places. Jack took the contact session, Les Cusworth the hands, Rex Hazeldine, the fitness expert, the sprint drills and Smurf — physio Kevin Murphy — the warm-up. This was a far better session than yesterday's and we kept to a very tight schedule. At 12.30 p.m., we boarded the team bus to a reception for lunch and at 1.30 we left the hotel for Heathrow to catch our flight to Dublin. The A team were on the same flight, so there was plenty of good-natured banter flying around. From Dublin Airport, we drove to Killiney Castle Hotel.

The next team meeting was at 7 p.m. Everyone was still very tense. We watched a video of the Irish pack, concentrating on their front row, which has received more rave reviews. Mooro was almost beside himself with rage by this time. Jack took the team meeting and Will concluded it. After a huge steak dinner, I went off down the road to a local pub with Kyran Bracken, Mike Catt, Dewi Morris, Jason Leonard, Jerry Guscott and Ben Clarke.

Friday 20 January

Another team meeting at 9.30 a.m. Snow on the hills behind Dublin, frozen grounds. Change of 10 a.m. training venue from Blackrock College to a comprehensive school way out of town. The ground was so hard we could only use half the pitch. Training was poor, with only a maximum of twenty minutes possible. To add to our problems, Johnno was still taking an extraordinarily long time to warm up because of his hamstring problem.

I spent the afternoon at the hotel, where I had my first session of acupuncture to try to get rid of my recurring scrum pox. I normally get it six or seven times a season, always after a game, which is probably because you are more prone to it when you are tired. Often it appears on the Tuesday after a Saturday match. Scrum pox is a virus and can be rather unpleasant. It's sometimes painful and you can get headaches from it as well. It is highly contagious, so I have to be careful around the house to make sure that my wife and daughter do not get infected.

The lad who does the massaging for the England team was at the hotel and mentioned he did acupuncture. He had his needles with him and suggested I tried it. It wasn't painful – I just lay there for about twenty minutes and that was it. I only had about three needles inserted into pressure points, but it relaxed me so much that I slept for three hours afterwards. And I have to reveal now that I was not to be troubled again by scrum pox for the rest of the season. Given that I have been suffering from it on and off since 1982, that is encouraging.

At the 7 p.m. meeting, Jack said a few words on why we should beat Ireland, but warned that we should expect a man-to-man battle. When it was over, Ben, Dewi and I wound up Mooro yet again about Wood. For the rest of that evening, we played chess and watched *The Word* before going to bed.

Saturday 21 January

Awoke to a howling gale and torrential rain. Everything over in Ireland always seems to go against us. Half an hour before the kick-off the rain miraculously ceased, but the wind was still horrendous. At least the pitch dried out pretty fast! Everybody was nervous about the game. You always are for the first match of the Championship, but especially for this fixture. Ireland in Dublin always contains an element of uncertainty. We knew we'd really be up against it, but we were fortunate enough to win the toss and play into the wind in the first half. We kept it very tight and nobody was under any illusions about what was required – just constant driving into the Irish and the elements, keeping it tight and never slacking in concentration.

We played very well in the first half. It was just a shame that we fell apart a little bit in the second: we got a bit too greedy in certain areas. I gave Rob Andrew a few strong words about where to put the ball and some of the media boys remarked on it afterwards. I will do that if it's necessary, and when I saw Rob trying to run the ball deep in our own half with the gale at our backs, I made it pretty clear where I wanted to be playing the game. The next kick from him boomed 65 yards downfield and we settled happily inside their 22. That was the place to play. In the end we won 20–8.

We had a great night afterwards, and the Irish were their usual hospitable selves, despite their defeat. Nicky, my wife, and a friend of ours visited friends in the Penthouse Suite of the Berkeley Court Hotel and then we went on to a nightclub somewhere in the city with other friends. Got back to the hotel about 4.30 a.m.

Saturday 28 January

Preparation for the Five Nations game against France began today, but first I played for Leicester against Bristol in the Pilkington Cup. We won the match 16-8, but I scratched the cornea of my right eye so Graham Rowntree, my Leicester forward colleague, had to drive me to Richmond to meet up with the rest of the squad. We had the usual team meeting at around 7 p.m., and this evening there were wild scenes of celebration when we heard that Jerry Guscott had at last scored a try to end his personal drought. So the old boy can still play after all.

Sunday 29 January

I couldn't train again, this time because of my eye. Drove home.

Wednesday 1 February

Back to Twickenham for a lunch in the Rose Room. The media are already billing this match once again as 'Le Crunch' and the attention was great. Had a 2–4.15 p.m. training session and then returned to the Petersham Hotel. I must have done something right as this time I have a room on my own. This was not at all usual until this year. Before that we always shared. In your own room you can do your own thing – watch what you want on TV or turn it off when you like, but funnily enough you do miss the camaraderie of a team-mate. Not that of the great snorers of our time, though. Jeff Probyn and Mike Teague were shockers.

The 7 p.m. team meeting was followed by dinner and then a visit to a local pub which had Sky TV, together with Mike Catt, Dewi, Johnno and Kyran. We stayed out a little too late really, and had an Indian meal on the way home. We got back about midnight in the end.

Thursday 2 February

Meeting at 9.30 a.m.; training session at 10, which was pretty uneventful. No injury scares, no pranks, but still a lot of media interest in us. We are feeling fairly confident but after such a winning streak as we've enjoyed against the French everybody is aware that it has to end some time. Not on Saturday, we hope. Early night.

Friday 3 February

The 10 a.m. meeting was followed by the usual light 10.30 a.m. Friday morning session. It's a chance just to get out, have a run and stretch your muscles. Nothing serious or heavy is done unless there is some special need because all the major work should have been completed by now. Had another session of acupuncture in the team room after lunch, and several of the boys said they felt squeamish at the sight. Everybody was still quite tense and the media are still paying us a lot of attention.

After the evening meeting we spent about an hour and a half doing all the autograph signings. There is always a mountain to do – rugby balls, shirts, cards, pictures, you name it. Some of the lads even get the odd jockstrap sent to them for signing!

After dinner, I went to the local cinema to watch *Road to Wellville* with Tim Rodber, while some of the others saw *Vampire* with Tom Cruise. Anything to kill the time, really. I was happy enough with this until I found out later that I'd missed out on a game of my favourite three-card brag.

Saturday 4 February

This wasn't the best French side we have ever met but they were probably the cleanest. Perhaps the outcome had something to do with that. All French teams I have played against have been Jekyll and Hyde characters: hard men on the field, very pleasant and well mannered off it. They did manage to score a typical, classic French try finished off by Viars, the substitute, but by then we were well in charge and I was pleased that several of the back-row moves came off well, especially the one which set up Tony Underwood for the last try. We had worked on that and it was very satisfying when it came off. Despite the three tries in our 31–10 victory, it wasn't a classic match, and we had a very quiet night.

Sunday 5 February

I drove home fairly early as I was due to start work at 3 p.m. That is tough but you get used to it, and in fairness, it happens only very occasionally. The people at work come from the Leicester area and are almost all strong Tigers rugby men, so they like to stop for a quick chat to find out how I got on.

Saturday 11 February

This was just not my day. Leicester had a hard Courage League match at Gloucester and we lost it 9–3 after playing poorly. In the middle of February, with Bath vying for another League title, the last thing you want to do is lose a game like this. But we England players had to jump in the car and drive up to Richmond for another England squad weekend before the Cardiff match next week. Halfway there, the car broke down so we were late arriving and missed the 7 p.m. meeting. So we went straight to the Sun, the famous rugby pub in Richmond, and ran into Ross Kemp, the actor who plays Grant Mitchell in *EastEnders*, and a Welsh referee who lived in Holland. He immediately lent us his red and yellow cards so that we could immediately send Ross off. It turned into a very late night which had repercussions. When we got back to the hotel, it was around 2 a.m. We were assuming that everyone else would be safely tucked up in bed and our late return would go unnoticed. But Kyran, who we'd met later in the Sun, saw that the TV was still on. He went into the team room to find Jack Rowell sitting there studying videos. It wasn't the ideal end to a day best forgotten.

Sunday 12 February

Training was very poor this morning. It was as if everyone was hung over. Jack Rowell stepped in after a while to express his dissatisfaction about the late night some of the players had had. It was a fair point. Yet sometimes training just doesn't go well anyway and it is hard to see why. It may be a good sign: players might be trying too hard and may be too tense because they're so keen to succeed. Alternatively, of course, it could just be because they've been out too late. Clearly in this case Jack thought it was the latter.

Wednesday 15 February

Met at the Bath Spa Hotel, where I'm rooming with Tim Rodber. Had a 'closed' training session at 2 p.m. in front of five hundred Bath University students in hail, wind and rain! At the evening team meeting Jack told us we had to lay to rest the Welsh jinx. He said there were videos available for us to watch so that we could see what we should do. Later that evening, a few of us went out to a local pub for a quiet drink but found a *News of the World* reporter lurking there. We moved on to another. This reporter had approached me after Leicester's match at Gloucester and asked if I'd do what he described as a 'fun article' wearing police gear. I declined, because I didn't think it would be in the best interests of the force.

Thursday 16 February

Team meeting at 9 a.m.; training at 10, again at Bath University – again in rain, hail and high winds. It was another closed session, and only about three hundred students turned up this time! It only lasted an hour and was not a particularly good session. That was the fault of the players and the weather, not the coaches.

We drove in convoy to Cardiff in the afternoon, but apart from Tony Underwood, whom I saw a few times, we all lost each other once we got on the motorway, conditions were so bad. Torrential rain fell the whole way. When we arrived, the Welsh were unusually polite, which we couldn't quite believe. In the past, they have sometimes been extremely rude, shouting and swearing at us on the streets in Cardiff. This time, it was very different. I think the years of losing have punctured some of Welsh rugby's arrogance.

Team meeting at 7 p.m.

Friday 17 February

Team meeting at 10, training at 10.30, and again the Welsh were most courteous and polite. The weather, on the other hand, was shocking with frequent hail showers. There were a few dropped balls and unforced errors because everyone was so nervous. Once the session was over, I returned to our hotel in the centre of Cardiff for lunch and another course of acupuncture.

After the inevitable team meeting I played three-card brag and lost a lot of money to Kyran Bracken on the last hand. He had a prial of 10s to my 1, 2 and 3 on the bounce.

Saturday 18 February

An early start as usual for me, at around 7 to 7.30 a.m. I had a light breakfast and then wandered into the team room, where Les Cusworth joined me. We discussed our game plan for about half an hour.

Given England's dire record in Cardiff, it didn't matter how we won the game and whether we produced good or bad rugby. We had to ensure we kept up the pressure on Wales and forced them into mistakes on which we could capitalize. On most of the last few visits to Cardiff, it has been England that have been forced into errors, with Wales taking advantage. This time, however, the boot was on the other foot, and although it wasn't a great game, it was the result we had come for. After our 23–9 win, we walked back to the team hotel and found that the Welsh had suddenly lost their politeness. Obscenities were shouted at us from across the street as we left the stadium. It was a shame, but it is no more than we have come to expect in Cardiff, and we had been somewhat sceptical about the earlier show of courtesies. Jerry and I ran into Mike Teague and Peter Winterbottom and arranged to meet them later in the evening. We left the official dinner halfway through and went for an Indian meal, but it was a fairly quiet night. Most of the official dinners are pretty boring. The Welsh and Irish ones aren't too bad, but the Scots' dinner is usually the worst.

Sunday 19 February

I drove back home from Cardiff feeling pretty tired. Three games gone, three wins under our belts . . . just one win to go and another Grand Slam will be clinched. The pressure is still right on us.

Wednesday 1 March

As we have had a weekend off, a training session was fitted in this evening at Marlow RFC, our usual midweek meeting place, as the build-up to the Grand Slam decider against Scotland at Twickenham begins. After a 6 a.m. to 2 p.m. police shift, I drove down to Buckinghamshire. It always means a lateish night for me – it is around midnight by the time I get home – but for someone like Dewi Morris, who comes down from Lancashire, it's terribly late. Often he doesn't get home until 2 a.m. – and he hasn't even been in the side this season. The boys definitely feel sorry for him.

Saturday 11 March

Today's training session was unique in that we had three very important visitors. Her Royal Highness the Princess of Wales and her two sons, Princes William and Harry, came to meet us and watch us working. Some of these occasions can be forced and awkward, but this one wasn't because the Princess is so natural and polite. You don't feel in the slightest bit uncomfortable chatting to her. All her bodyguards stayed discreetly in the background and we had a pleasant chat. Afterwards, just to bring us back to reality there was ... yes, you've guessed it, another 7 p.m. team meeting.

Sunday 12 March

Team meeting: 9.30 a.m.; training session: 10 a.m. This was an open session, with the media present. Sometimes we find the media too intrusive. Cameras start encroaching on to the pitch and they get in the way. The cameramen seem to want to try and photograph scrums from underneath to get the faces close up and things like that. It's hard to have a proper training session in those conditions. After training, we went off to meet the winners of some competitions, including one run by Cellnet, in the Obolensky Suite at Twickenham. Then came the drive home followed by a long 5 p.m. to 2 a.m. night shift.

Wednesday 15 March

A Courage lunch 12 noon at the Bank of England ground followed by training from 2 to 4 p.m. Once again the enormous media presence was a distraction. Graham Dawe injured a calf muscle in the session which has meant a call-up for Greg Botterman of Saracens to back up Brian Moore, as the A team was in Durban to play Natal. I stayed in this evening. Everyone seems pleased that at last there is only one match to go in the Five Nations competition. The pressure and commitments of the season have been huge.

Thursday 16 March

Team meeting at 9.30 a.m.; 10 a.m.: closed training session, followed by an afternoon of watching videos to try to pick up some clues as to the way the Scots play.

Another team meeting at 7 p.m. followed by a quiet evening at the hotel.

Friday 17 March

Team meeting at 10, a light training run at 10.30. Then back to the hotel for another acupuncture session and a haircut at Gino's in the afternoon. There is still a strong general feeling of wanting to get the match over with. But we all feel that we won't lose, or at least, that if we do, it will only be because of what we have failed to do rather than because Scotland have produced anything sensational to surprise us.

After the evening team meeting there was a game of three-card brag, which I won this time.

Saturday 18 March

Grand Slam showdown day. The media have made much of the so-called revenge clash after Scotland beat us to the Grand Slam in 1990, but that was five long years ago and things are different now. We went out at 11 a.m. for a line-out session to go through a few moves and calls.

The game itself was very dour and intense. I injured a rib, suffering a sprung cartilage, and had to come off with twenty minutes to go. We didn't play as well as we could have done but it was very difficult to be expansive in a game that was so tight and tense. In the end, Rob Andrew's kicking punished the Scots for their mistakes, scoring all our 24 points to Scotland's 12, and we won that way. I spoke to Rob Wainwright afterwards and it seemed that Scotland's only game plan had been to hoist the high ball and try to force mistakes from us; to try to disrupt us all the while. They certainly achieved that, and Brian Moore made it clear afterwards what he thought of it all. They *did* come to kill our possession and to prevent us from playing to our strengths. Perhaps most teams try to do that to some extent these days, but in Scotland's case I think they knew that it was their only chance of winning.

We were more relieved than ecstatic afterwards at having won the Grand Slam. The season has been so exhausting that it has probably taken the gloss off it all. It was still great to do what we did, of course, but it has become almost like a job nowadays. The approach to it all has changed so much. In 1991, we were desperate to win a Grand Slam but this year we always had the feeling that whatever we did in the Five Nations, we were only halfway through the year because of the World Cup looming in June. We had the mentality that another six or seven matches remained before the end of the season proper in South Africa. Everything we have done this year was with the World Cup in mind rather than the Five Nations. By the end of today's match, there was just an overriding sense of relief that the job had been completed, nothing more. The majority of the after-match nights this season have been very quiet because we know the ultimate challenge awaits us further down the road. Not even tonight was an exception. We had a very low-key evening considering the fact that we have just won the Grand Slam Five Nations Championship, Triple Crown and Calcutta Cup.

Sunday 19 March

Morning. I awoke feeling pretty sore and I knew there was no way I could go to work today. So I did what I never like doing – rang the station to call in sick due to the rib injury. I was due on duty at 3 p.m. today, but instead, we drove steadily back home. Closing the door on the 1995 Championship does not seem to have come a moment too soon.

7 Amateurism: The Great Debate

Money and rugby: two words which increasingly seem to go hand in hand in the game – or at least they do in some people's minds. Let me make it clear at the very outset that I am not one of those people. I am not in any sense motivated by money – to me, it cannot begin to compare with the enjoyment of playing the game, the company of those I meet through my association with the sport and the friendships made. Many rugby friendships seem to last a lifetime, if those of previous generations are a reliable indicator. Frankly, I have never looked for anything else from the game.

I went into Rugby Union fully aware that it was a truly amateur sport, and I have always been perfectly happy to adhere strictly to the rules of amateurism. They were laid down years ago and seemed fair and reasonable. Throughout the main part of my career I can honestly say that I have never really been very interested in the topic of money in the game. Of course, I have been aware of others taking a more active role in pursuing financial reward, from as far back as my experiences in France. Nothing much has changed there – players received money years ago and probably still do. It is an accepted part of the game there, for better or worse.

It just so happens that in England that has never been the case. Countries like England and Ireland have stood like a rock against the growing tide of money sweeping ever faster into the sport. Or at least (in the case of England anyway), they have resisted specific invasions of finance, namely those aimed at rewarding players. In the matter of welcoming huge funds to swell the coffers of the Rugby Football Union (RFU) and to develop Twickenham into one of the world's greatest sports grounds, they have adopted a quite different approach.

Sponsors have been warmly embraced and welcomed into the fold to deposit their millions of pounds into the RFU's bank accounts. Some commercial firms have doubtless been very pleased indeed with the results of their involvement; others, I imagine, might have been less delighted at what they have got out of it. But the basic point is this: those who organize and administrate the game have brought it out of the old days when it was truly and thoroughly amateur into a situation where it is now, in some respects, a commercial giant intent on making as much money as possible. They did this to bring it into the twentieth century and make its appeal as widespread as possible. Developing the game as a whole to compete with other sports was undoubtedly one of their reasons for doing so.

But they must understand that what they have spawned is a very different attitude to a transformed game. Those in authority must acknowledge that it was not the players who provided this momentum for change, it was the administrators themselves. No England player went out and persuaded a business to give him material reward until those companies had been signed up by the RFU. They were already on board, and their money was already swilling around the system.

As these events have unfolded, I have become more interested in such matters, and the debate on the subject within rugby circles has increased because the demands and expectations of these sponsoring companies have affected clubs and players themselves. Any player with a senior club and international side will tell you that the growing commercialization of the sport has changed his life almost beyond recognition. Never before has so much been demanded of players, and gradually they have looked at this situation and asked for a slice of the cake themselves. No one can be surprised at that. Nor, in my view, is it wrong for people who are contributing so much to the general wellbeing of the game to expect some reward for all their efforts. We live in a totally different sporting environment in 1995. Thirty years ago, players trained twice a week with their clubs and if they were chosen for internationals, they usually turned up the afternoon before a match and had a preliminary chat about it over a couple of beers in the bar on a Friday night. The standards now required dictate that most players must train virtually every day of the week; either that, or play almost every week to keep in trim.

It is hardly astonishing, then, that some friction has developed over the union's reluctance to allow the players to benefit from this financial development as some compensation for their commitment. It has been the view of the majority of England players in recent years that the union has attempted to prevent us from enjoying any proper financial package. There has been prevarication and delay, obfuscation and apparently deliberate blocking of a system that would operate for our real benefit.

The question of monetary rewards for players started to surface long ago. I can remember at the start of the 1989 British Lions tour of Australia some of the Scottish Lions telling everyone that they had to make the most of the situation from a commercial point of view, and that meant charging for any interviews we did with the Australian media. Most reporters in this part of the world will tell you that I have never so much as mentioned any form of reward for giving an interview. Admittedly I don't do many, but that is because sitting down and pouring out my thoughts on any subject is not something I enjoy. It is not because of arrogance or anything like that. I prefer to let others do the talking and just get on with my game. Nevertheless, under this gentle pressure from some of the Scottish lads with the Lions, the other squad members reluctantly agreed to ask for some payment. Unfortunately, the first people to be interviewed were myself, Wade Dooley and Paul Ackford. When we went outside and I said to this Australian guy, 'Right, you want to interview us, but how much are you going to give us?' I felt about as comfortable as Martin Bayfield would have done going walking in size 6 shoes.

The guy looked as embarrassed as us, but all the same he offered to lob forty or fifty dollars into the players' kitty. The three of us had no idea whether this represented huge generosity, appalling stinginess or just about the going rate. Anyway, we said, fine, and that seemed to be it – until the next day's Australian newspapers plastered the story all over their pages with the headline:

British trio ask for money.

It was the only time I had ever been in that situation and I had come an enormous cropper.

To a lesser extent, that kind of situation has been repeated because of the failure of the RFU to agree a deal with the England players whereby a joint enterprise could be set up from which the players could benefit financially for promotional work. We as individuals have been forced to go our own way and do our own thing in this field, and it is my belief that both sides have suffered as a result.

Until the staggering news that Will Carling had been sacked as England captain hit the headlines on the morning of the 1995 Cup final, I was of the firm opinion that both parties were to blame for the impasse which had gradually grown up between the players and the administrators of the Rugby Football Union. It seemed to me to come down to a problem between personalities – namely, Dudley Wood, the now retired secretary of the RFU, and Brian Moore, the England hooker and chief spokesman on the players' commercial affairs.

I doubt that I was alone in believing that there should have been a compromise. English rugby has seen an outstanding era in which Grand Slams and Triple Crowns have been won, a magnificent new stadium built and all kinds of ventures at a lower level in the game funded by the vast amounts of sponsorship money. Surely it should have been within the capabilities of those involved, both on the RFU and among the players, to have got together and hammered out an agreement. I thought the trouble was that the two people who were negotiating for each side were very stubborn people. Brian Moore can be dogmatic and normally he gets what he wants. But if he doesn't, he can find it very difficult to bend, and I think Dudley Wood was exactly the same.

By presiding over a continuing disagreement which dragged on for years and became increasingly messy and unpleasant, I think the RFU lost a lot of respect. You only have to look at how the dispute has been handled by the media. It is my impression that a lot of the general public and players from lower clubs tended to view the RFU as a bunch of old fuddy-duddies, which was unfortunate for those in authority. Personally, I didn't then think that that image was fair. There are some very nice people in the RFU, many of whom are quite in tune with what is going on. Those men understand the views of the players and several have sympathized with them. But because of the way the whole thing was reported and the issue handled by the two sides, people got the wrong idea about it. As a consequence, misconceptions arose about both positions on the matter.

Some people claim vigorously that the players are greedy. I don't accept this, although before the Will Carling affair I did think we were probably in the wrong in not trying a different approach once the negotiations failed initially in 1991. I thought we should have gone back to the negotiating table and asked them for something slightly different. Even if it had meant settling for something less than what we wanted, I thought we would have later got a lot more than we had bargained over in those days. There was definitely an opportunity after the 1991 World Cup, going towards the 1992 Five Nations Championship, to sort out this dispute. Sadly, the chance was not taken.

I didn't want to lay the blame at Brian Moore's door, he did a tremendous job in setting up Playervision, a company to look after the interests of the players, along with Rob Andrew and Will Carling. But as in everything, you have to be slightly flexible and, to me, neither party seemed to be. I knew that

Dudley Wood was certainly extremely stubborn, but he also had a sense of humour, and if you could get on the right side of him and get on with him as a person, then I thought you should have been able to find a way to address the problems. Perhaps the players would not have come away with absolutely everything we wanted, but in all negotiations you have to compromise somewhere.

However, in the light of Will's temporary sacking, news of which broke so spectacularly just a couple of weeks before the England squad departed for the 1995 World Cup finals in South Africa, I changed my mind on this whole question of the inability of the RFU officers and the England players to find common ground. Stubbornness is maybe one of Brian Moore's characteristics, but no one can any longer be in much doubt as to where the chief blame must lie for the failure to strike an agreement.

Having been involved, as were all the England players, in the affair of Will and the captaincy, I am now quite clear in my own mind where the seat of the problem was. When people reflect on the decision which the RFU committee made about Carling, they will begin to understand the struggle we have had in trying to find a solution to the differences. I no longer believe that it was six of one and half a dozen of the other. The whole business brought home to me just how archaic and behind the times the leading officers of the RFU really are. To me, the affair smelled strongly of a vendetta against Will. It was hard to interpret it in any other way.

The players were at first incredulous and then very upset at the action of the RFU. It was a distraction we could well have done without so close to our departure for South Africa. On the evening of the announcement I talked to Rob Andrew and we both agreed that if asked neither of us would take on the captaincy. There is no question that Will was the best man to captain England. In fact, the players would have gone to the World Cup without a skipper had the RFU not backed down, and perhaps when the RFU realized that, they felt that another look at the situation was appropriate. We thought that a polite request for them to reconsider was the best option.

Some might put the amateurism argument down to the inevitable birth pangs of a new system within rugby, but I wouldn't agree with that. Other countries – Australia and New Zealand, for example – have not had these problems, so why have England? It does not help that too many of those now in administration just do not understand the commitment required of modern-day players, especially those involved at international level. Did Dudley Wood ever play for England? Does he really appreciate, coming from another generation, what it takes to do so nowadays? I find it quite strange that someone should have such power, wield such authority over what international players should and should not be able to do, when he has not been there himself. There are people on the RFU who are forward-thinking, and we need those people, and a mix of individuals from different eras who have differing points of view, to decide official policy.

Where the RFU have fallen down in recent years is to have allowed one person who was very set in his ways to influence the decisions that were to be made when he has not been there or directly experienced the commitment that people have given to the game. I think that was wrong, and I believe a great many outsiders with no particular axe to grind will probably agree with me. After all, we were not asking for the earth, for enormous percentages of these million-pound deals the RFU were doing with companies. We just felt entitled to some reward. In no way were we being excessively greedy.

Plainly, too, the administrators at Twickenham had the time to set up and organize a system to give the players some benefit. Dudley was a paid employee of the RFU: had he wanted to, I am sure he or his colleagues could have found time to instigate something. In view of their silence they cannot be surprised at the gulf that opened up. I don't know whether Dudley Wood was as abrupt and rude as Brian alleged he was, but whatever the reason was, communication broke down badly.

Taking advantage of commercial opportunities means different things to different players. Jeremy Guscott is inevitably going to be in greater demand than Dean Richards or Jason Leonard because the backs will always get more exposure than the forwards in rugby. It is the way the game is. The try-scorers will always get the attention, just as the goal-scorers do in soccer, or the players who get the touch-downs in American football. You get used to it if you play a team sport. It might be a little disconcerting that some players get more money than others when you consider yourselves to be a team, but the tries have got to be scored, and if you have that touch of class then maybe you deserve it. It doesn't bother me at all if the backs get recognition while the forwards don't, although I know it worries some people.

Whether the commercial climate will change now that Tony Hallett has replaced Dudley Wood at Twickenham, it is probably too early to say. But if the stalemate continues (and as of August 1995 so much remained up in the air), we will carry on using the same company to promote us through individual sponsorship deals. That is not the option I would prefer, and I don't think I am alone in that view. The company involved has done a solid job and cannot be blamed for any failure, but the fact remains that this system takes up a lot of time and effort that we could be using more profitably on other things. Life could be made a whole lot easier for the England players and the RFU should know that already. If they don't, well, they will do now.

As for the future, it is my firm conviction that if an agreement is not reached English rugby will begin to suffer noticeably. New players would have to take over the roles Brian and Rob created and I think they would struggle to manage being rugby players for club and country and the level of involvement required in setting up commercial deals. There are only so many hours in a day. I believe that eventually we will arrive at a situation whereby rugby players are paid a lump sum to represent their country in each international. Not only is it bound to happen, but the sooner it does, the better, I'd say. You could have bonuses on top of that for loyalty, so that a player pulling on an international jersey for, say, the twentieth, or thirtieth, or fortieth, or fiftieth time would receive an extra amount as he reached the relevant milestone. You would have to negotiate the bonus system to ensure that it was worked out fairly.

The ideal scenario would be for the RFU to employ the players to promote rugby, paying them a lump sum at the start and end of each season. It would stop the exploitation of individuals and make commercial involvement a team thing – and I'd like to think that the commitment required by the RFU would not be so great as to disrupt families or ordinary careers. Some say that if this solution were adopted it would lead to the soul of the game being lost. That is not true. Other countries have gone this far down the road to commercialization without any apparent damage to the basis of the sport. In fact, in some of those countries the game is positively thriving.

It seems clear to me that the only way to go forward is to have the RFU directing financial rewards for players so that the status quo between the players and committee can be maintained. Developments have been taking place at a much quicker pace in the southern hemisphere countries, but I fear that there may still be enough people in high places within the RFU, even now that Dudley Wood has gone, who may cling on to his views in the hope of delaying real change for even longer. For the players this can only be disheartening, especially when they see their New Zealand counterparts advertising cars and other products on national television in their country and coming off rugby pitches biting into Mars bars in front of the cameras. The Australians are being signed up by their union and guaranteed a set sum of money, even if they suffer injury and miss matches: the Packer affair in July 1995 hastened all this. There is no animosity towards or envy of the southern hemisphere players because they have got things organized as they should be. Frustration is the word that sums up our feelings, and the fact that we are prevented from doing similar deals makes us think badly of the RFU. The essence of this whole affair is that we are not operating on a level playing field.

I see countries like these dragging England into the modern world eventually, but sadly it will take other nations to lead the way before England will follow. That is a pity, because it would be nice to settle this ongoing problem once and for all. There is no doubt that it is a distraction to the players and that it can cause friction. It is not my intention to overdramatize the point, but when some players turn up for England training without the right training shirts or shoes and get ticked off for it, the seeds of disharmony are sown. The players are not all equally commercially minded and some of us don't appreciate being told what we can or cannot wear. I can see that if the specified gear is not worn you risk damaging the contract with the sponsors, but I, for one, like to feel comfortable, to wear what I wish to wear. I have accepted such stipulations because I want to be part of the team and sometimes in these circumstances you have to compromise, but on occasions it can go a little too far. Commercialism is always there at the back of the players' minds. People are always thinking, 'What are we going to do next?' and 'What should we be doing to please the sponsors?' I do not believe that is how international teams should be thinking, however brief the attention given to these matters. If the RFU organized the commercial aspects for the players themselves, that problem would be solved for us.

I don't claim to have been deeply involved in commercial interests. At times they can be a hindrance in the build-up to a match. You might have photos to do, or lunches or receptions to attend, when all you want to do is focus on the match itself. I prefer to do my own thing. I like to get the preparation for a game right in my own mind and to make sure I am ready and in the best possible condition, both mentally and physically, by myself. I don't rely on others – I just don't need to have someone else shouting encouragement at me or trying to gee me up before a game. I don't think fringe distractions should occupy our minds in the days leading up to a match, but they have crept on to the schedule because we have been left to get on with them ourselves, without RFU assistance. You couldn't say that we have actually lost an international because of the squad's involvement in commercial interests a few days earlier, but the fact remains that some squad players have found certain commitments hampering and even one appointment of that nature is one too many.

If the RFU really marketed the team and ran the show, I cannot see any reason why future England players could not be paid a basic lump sum of several thousand pounds for each season with a bonus system on top. How would it help the players? It would greatly improve the relationship between an employer and an employee involved in rugby at a senior level, for a start.

If such a system had been in operation prior to the World Cup, I would have been in a position to go to my employers, the Police Federation, and ask for four months' unpaid leave leading up to and including the tournament. Look at it from the point of view of the police. They could employ a temporary replacement for me or pay others overtime as cover if they were not paying my salary. As it was, instead of concentrating on preparation for the World Cup and the major England matches which preceded it in the Five Nations Championship, I was trying to fit in rugby training sessions and matches, shift work for the police – which often involved nights – as well as time off with my family. It was all but impossible. The demands of rugby alone are now immense. As an England player and captain of Leicester in 1994–5, I had to spend time on such things as personal training, club training, phone calls to other players and club officials to keep up with events at Welford Road, visits to other players, helping organization at the club and discussing all sorts of matters.

If the reluctance in the England set-up to help financially does not change, I am convinced that players will just burn out of the system much earlier than has ever been the case before. In this respect rugby would follow the example of professional soccer in that the lifespan of the top players would be reduced by continuing commitments. The other danger is that people will sort out their own sponsorship deals and move away from the RFU and its auspices.

Of course, the bottom line on all of this is that in a few years' time it will be only briefly remembered. By then, I'm sure, players will be receiving lump-sum payments for international rugby while the sport continues to flourish and everyone gets on with spreading the game even further around the world without the distraction of petty squabbles over whether players can advertise England shirts or appear in their own sponsored boots. In time, what has happened in the last three or four years will come to be seen as a storm in a teacup.

However, while that situation is almost certain to exist at international level, I am by no means as sure that most clubs will ever be able to pay their players. Some are already paying their best people and always will, but they may find it increasingly hard to do so with all the costs involved with running a rugby club. At Leicester, as I've said, no player has ever been paid, although there were suggestions around August 1995 that this might change. The situation had suddenly become very fluid owing to the Kerry Packer affair.

Clubs like ours are required to spend vast amounts of money on getting their grounds up to standards compatible with their standing in the game. Then they have to finance the modern-day facilities at their training grounds. In the last twelve or eighteen months Leicester have spent a considerable sum on their Oadby training ground, putting in such things as an Astroturf surface to make possible training in all weathers, floodlighting on three pitches, scrummaging machines, a new gymnasium and new shower rooms. They are also engaged in building a new stand at Welford Road and upgrading facilities in general around the ground, such as in the clubhouse, which is being extended. All this will swallow up a vast amount of money — anything from two million to five million pounds by the time the whole project is completed – so it is not hard to see why the club has always resisted the idea of paying its players.

The only way I can see a club like the Tigers financing such an arrangement is by attracting a sponsor to put up the money solely for the players. But then would you not be playing for a company as much as for your club? I don't know that I would want that, and I'm not sure the other players would either.

Leicester offer their players a lot already. They provide us with the best facilities in the country as far as first-class clubs go and the back-up of talent in terms of coaching and administration is extensive. The club and the players get together and set up some sponsorship work which involves us going to events and functions, sometimes just to meet people or perhaps to make a speech. Funds are raised for a central pool in this way and at the end of the day most of the players benefit in some shape or form. The beauty of it is that we are not taking money out of the club.

If local sponsors want to offer us money to play in their boots or to wear their shirts, then fair enough. I don't believe that causes any damage to the structure of the game at club or international level. The only danger is if one player gets more than another and internal squabbling starts, but that doesn't happen at Leicester. If you do anything, my advice is to do it as a team, not as individuals, at club level. This is not something that has affected me very much because I am restricted in what I can do by the police, who do not allow people to have outside business interests unless they are agreed in advance with the force. I want to be in the police force so I have no problem with that. It does not rule out every activity for me – I can do certain promotional work.

The last point to make on the subject is that the rewards available are pretty small in any case. We are not talking telephone numbers here for anyone. Some of the younger players who came into the England squad expecting to earn quite a lot of money got a real shock. The reality is that even some quite well-known figures don't earn that much.

Because of my lesser involvement in the commercial face of rugby, I think I have been able to take a slightly more detached view than some. And whatever the rights and wrongs, I believe English rugby would have been a great deal better off if there had been agreement between the two sides a long, long time ago. Now, however, it seems that in the light of events in the summer of 1995 things are going to move forward pretty fast. Perhaps now the RFU are regretting their previous refusal to assist the players in a scheme, for it seems as though the dam may suddenly have burst.

8 Life with the Lions

When I reflect on my involvement with the British Lions, both real and in my imagination, a sense of frustration creeps over me. I was lucky enough to be part of two British Lions tours, those of 1989 and 1993, but I was also disappointed not to have had the opportunity to make an earlier tour: the planned 1986 trip to South Africa, which was called off because of the political situation in that country.

Lions tours in the 1980s were subject to some distinctly strange timing. Until 1983, the British Isles used to tour a particular country every six years. In that year, they returned to New Zealand exactly six years after their last visit there, the ill-fated 1977 trip which was ruined by the weather. The 1983 tour, on the other hand, was ruined by the results – New Zealand whitewashed the Lions 4–0 in the series. In between there had been a 1980 visit to South Africa and another trip was scheduled there for 1986, the usual three-year gap after the previous Lions tour. I was a newcomer to international rugby that year, having won my first caps for England in that season's Five Nations Championship against Ireland and France. There was much speculation as to the likely make-up of the Lions party had the tour gone ahead. Now, I am not one to devote a great deal of time to pondering on hypothetical situations – generally, I am a person who prefers to get on with his life and face reality – but I was intrigued when one leading commentator, asked to list the thirty players he thought would have comprised that year's Lions squad, selected Scotland's John

Beattie and myself as his No. 8s. As events turned out, I had to wait three more years before I was chosen.

With South Africa off the map in terms of Lions tours, a first-ever full tour of Australia alone was organized for 1989.

This was a radical departure for the British Isles because they had never before toured Australia alone. Parties heading for New Zealand used to stop off in Australia in the days of boats, flying boats and then old-fashioned, comparatively slow aircraft to play some warm-up games there. The Australians were never considered strong enough to host a full Lions tour, so you had teams like the 1966 Lions playing seven or eight games in Australia before they even got to New Zealand for the main tour. In those days players were away for months on a major tour and only those fortunate enough to be able to be away for such a long time would go. For today's players it would be impossible to take so much leave from work.

In 1989 there were, I think it is fair to say, many people who still doubted the worth of a full Lions tour to Australia itself, arguing that, apart from the Test matches and the games against two states, Queensland and New South Wales, there would be no teams to provide real competition for the Lions. I was prepared to delay judgement until I had experienced at first hand what the Aussies had to offer. But before that there was the thrill of hearing the news that, yes, I was in the squad. Some pundits might have forecast that I'd be chosen, as they do in the week or so prior to the announcement of the touring party. But you never know for sure until you actually hear it on the radio or TV, and even then you can't quite believe it until the official invitation plops through your letterbox.

That Lions badge still means a great deal to players and I felt a considerable pride at my selection for the 1989 tour. It was, too, the ideal tonic to buck me up after the disappointment every English player had felt at the close of that year's Five Nations tournament. We had experienced a real rollercoaster season, starting off with a thumping 28–19 win over the touring Australians at Twickenham. But our optimism was short-lived

– in the New Year Scotland held us to a 12–12 draw at Twickenham in our Five Nations opening game and our four penalty goals were little consolation after the four tries we had scored against the Aussies.

We fared rather better in our next match, beating Ireland in Dublin, which is never the easiest thing to do, by a 16–3 margin. Our next game was at home to France, whom we had not beaten since 1982. That meant a run of five defeats and a draw in six games against them – a far cry from the record we then put together. Our discipline in that 1989 match was near impeccable – we took what the French had to throw at us and kept our minds firmly on the task in front of us to secure an 11–0 win – and we haven't lost to them since.

It meant that if we beat Wales in Cardiff in our last match we would win the Championship, no matter what France did against Scotland in Paris. In the event, we had a dreadful time on a dreadful day at Cardiff, making a series of mistakes and losing 12–9. The Championship title had gone and one of the men most instrumental in our defeat, the Welsh scrum-half Robert Jones, was promptly chosen for the Lions tour. He deserved it. His high, hanging kicks had destroyed us in Cardiff that day. I was not in the least bit surprised that the Lions selectors decided they could not do without him in Australia.

Another Welshman who had a significant hand in our demise in Cardiff, lock Robert Norster, was also selected for the tour – six years after he'd been on the Lions trip to New Zealand. Five other Welshmen were picked – a surprise, perhaps, given that Wales had finished bottom of the table in the Championship – Ieuan Evans, Mike Hall and John Devereux among the backs and Mike Griffiths and Dai Young in the forwards. But the greatest concentration of players came from England and Scotland. This was perhaps inevitable in view of the fact that the two sides had tied for second place in the Five Nations table. There were nine Scots: both full-backs in Gavin Hastings and Peter Dods; Scott Hastings, Craig Chalmers and Gary Armstrong in the backs and up front David Sole and their entire back row, John Jeffrey, Finlay Calder and Derek White. Ten Englishmen toured: Rory Underwood, Chris Oti and Jerry Guscott among the threequarters (Will Carling was ruled out by a shin-splints injury) and in the forwards, Brian Moore, Gareth Chilcott, Wade Dooley, Paul Ackford, Mike Teague, Andy Robinson and myself. Four Irishmen completed the tour party: backs Brendan Mullin and Paul Dean, and Steve Smith and Donal Lenihan in the pack.

There were some notable omissions, the most serious being Jeff Probyn, England's tight-head prop forward. He had just spent the Five Nations season more than holding his own against such renowned scrummagers as France's Pascal Ondarts, hardly a weak link in any scrum. Probyn was to my mind the master tight head – strong, solid, reliable and destructive. I could not remember seeing a better tight head anywhere in Britain. The tight head is the fulcrum of any scrum, a key man. He stays in the scrummage the longest, holding it tight and ensuring stability. If your tight head is under pressure, you are in severe difficulties and the back row have no platform whatsoever from which to operate. Probyn had consistently shown what a tough customer he was, and I could not believe it when I heard he had been overlooked by the Lions selectors.

The problem was that he had been concussed in the match against Ireland in Dublin. He was replaced by Gareth Chilcott of Bath, who stayed in the England side for the rest of the season and was then selected ahead of Probyn for the Lions. Coochie was certainly a very capable player, but I did not regard him in the same light as a thoroughly destructive tight head. And as it turned out, Coochie had problems on the tour with his calf and was troubled by it for much of the time. If we'd known then what we know now, the selectors might have picked Probyn instead. But whether it was Coochie who should have just missed out or someone else is not for me to say. What I do know is that Probyn should have gone as the first-choice tight-head prop. If you look at what he could achieve in a scrummaging sense it was unbelievable. His scrummaging was second to none in the world, and in my eyes, he was never pushed back. He has always had this extraordinary ability to turn and twist, which makes it impossible for the opposition scrum to drive through him. In the southern hemisphere you always need your scrum to be as sound as possible. If there was one person in the whole of the British Isles who could assure you of that stability in the scrum, it would have been Probyn. Everyone must have known that.

But Probyn was not just a great scrummager: I have always found him a real pain in the arse as an opponent. If there was any loose ball he would be there trying to pick it up. He was always one of those people who would get in the way. I don't know whether he did it deliberately or not, but whatever the reason he is always difficult to play against. He has never got the credit for the work he did off the ball.

As for the line-out, you only have to ask Paul Ackford what Probes could do there. He is a tremendous line-out support player. We used to have a move with England whereby I would pop round the front of the line-out and Ackford would go to the back. Nobody could believe I had jumped like I had done for the ball. It was the support of Probyn which had me leaping like a salmon. You had to get off the ground initially, of course, but once you were airborne Probyn would get into a position where he would support you and give you that extra lift. He could hold up a bloke of even my weight. He is a unique person in rugby circles and a unique character, and we still get on very well. I find Jeff a lovely person, although I'd hate to be someone who has crossed him because when he dislikes people, he really dislikes them. He's a strange breed in that, in his mind, what is black is black and what is white is white. There is nothing in between. But he is an uncomplicated guy and if you are honest with him he will be the same with you.

I wanted Probes to be on that 1989 Lions tour because, having toured Australia the year before with England and experienced defeat in the Test matches by 22–16 and 28–8, I knew we would be up against it. The sides England had encountered out there were very good and extremely well balanced. The Australians at that time did not seem just to go for huge packs. They all seemed to choose well-balanced sides.

The Lions further compounded their initial difficulties by setting off with only one recognized openside flanker, Andy Robinson of Bath. Finlay Calder, the captain, could play on the left or right, but he had not been renowned throughout his career as a genuine openside.

For a considerable part of the early weeks of the tour, it was not a happy trip. The rivalry which had been steadily building up between England and Scotland in the Five Nations Championship spilled over into a 'them and us' situation on the tour. To say that we did not really get on would not be telling lies; there was real friction between us. It took at least five or six of the twelve matches we played, almost half the tour, for us to bury the hatchet and combine to work for the greater good. That discord came very close to costing us success in the Test series.

The Scots felt they knew best what sort of game was required and the English felt similarly – except that their game plan was quite different. The animosity never actually spilled over into a fight but there were a few verbal wars at team meetings. We were very far from the kind of cohesive, determined unit which ought to produce a sort of 'all together, lads' feeling and reaction. There were too many arguments for that. One group would ask, 'Why can't we do it this way?' and the other would retort 'Because we're doing it our way.' When we began the tour, the Scottish method prevailed. There was a Scottish coach, Ian McGeechan, with England's Roger Uttley as his assistant. The strong partnership between coach and captain, McGeechan and Calder, got its way, to start with, at least. But a fair majority of the forwards were English, and it was alien to us to play the driving, rucking type of game which the Scots used constantly. The English pack much preferred a mauling style, and the two were just incompatible. I felt that, having toured previously in Australia and played four internationals against them, the

English boys were better equipped, and perhaps understood better what was required to beat the Aussies, than the Scots, who had not toured there for some time. Furthermore, the New Zealand and Scottish game plans were very similar in their rucking style, and we felt that the Australians would be able to counter a rucking game more easily, having played so many matches in the Bledisloe Cup against New Zealand.

We started the tour with six straight wins, but the results of the matches against the traditionally strong sides were close. We beat Queensland 19–15 in Brisbane and New South Wales 23–21 in Sydney. Australia B were also defeated quite narrowly, by 23–18, but the other games were more predictable. And so we came to the First Test, and we had problems. Mike Teague wasn't well, so we were forced to restructure the back row with Derek White playing on the blindside flank, Finlay Calder at openside and myself at No. 8. This was a far from ideal combination. We desperately needed a well-balanced back row, but this one was made up of a blindside flanker and two No. 8s. Not surprisingly, we were exposed for it.

Looking back, it shouldn't have come as a great surprise that we lost the First Test. We were disorganized, we lost people the day before who might have played, and going into the match, we weren't really sure what everyone's individual role was meant to be. The defeat, and it was a pretty convincing one by the end at 30–12, really shook us up. We were not ready for the game, and fair credit to the Australians, they showed us up for what we were – a divided, ill-equipped squad which was not pulling together and did not seem capable of containing them. If you lose the First Test in a four-match series, you are in trouble. Lose the first of a three-Test series and you are staring down a shotgun barrel.

It was a shattering defeat, but in the end it was the making of the tour. We realized that now our backs were up against the wall and knew we had to play our hearts out in every game. The turning point of the whole trip came four days later in Canberra. Australian Capital Territory stormed into a big lead, fifteen points or more as I remember. Those of us who had played in the beaten Test side the previous Saturday wore expressions of near despair. If the Wednesday side started to lose too, it would be a titanic task to revive the tour. It is not often recognized by the public that the performances of the mid-week, or so-called second-string team are frequently an important factor in the success of the first-choice side on a tour. If the 'reserves' keep winning they raise the morale of the entire party. If they lose, there is even more pressure on the first team. This point was to be emphasized with brutal clarity in New Zealand four years later.

In 1989 we knew that only a win for the midweek side would lift the morale that had been so badly dented among the entire squad by the Test defeat. Now the reserves dug deep and took on ACT to claw back the big deficit and emerge winners by 41–25. The value of that victory was incalculable and the whole party owed a mighty debt to Donal's Doughnuts, as the midweek team had been known ever since the Irish lock Donal Lenihan had been given the captaincy. It was a rousing perform-ance, and it led to a resolution of the smouldering dispute between the Scots and the English.

We probably all knew, deep down, that if that rivalry per-sisted we would return home losers. There was no way a dis-united squad could turn round so tough a situation. It was fascinating to watch the party truly come together as it needed to do. Socially, the players had mixed before, but there was always this undercurrent of the difference of opinion as to which way we should play. We couldn't come to an agreement before the First Test, but once we lost that the English boys decided that the team would use the style we were used to. The Scots had had their turn, and we'd failed. Now it was our chance to see if our method would work better.

There was another factor which helped us salvage the tour: the outpourings of the Australian media. When we arrived in Australia, we were immediately dubbed 'Grandad's Team' or 'Dad's Army'. When we started to win games and beat some of the better teams, some people changed their tune and decided that perhaps we weren't so bad after all. But when we lost the First Test it was as though the whole of the Australian media had ganged up and returned to the Dad's Army theme. This helped considerably to get us hyped up for the Second Test.

The media wrote things about us on that tour of which they ought to be ashamed. Some of their comments were bordering on libellous, others were just absurd. They had almost questioned whether we were real men. After the First Test I received some stitches in my lip and there was much speculation in the Australian press as to how I'd been injured. It was said that Brian Moore or Bob Norster had been swinging back to throw a fist at an Australian and had instead caught me. It was typical of the Australian press to write something like that when all that had happened was that Brian had gone to strike for the ball in a scrum, the scrum had collapsed and his feet had flipped up and caught me in the mouth.

I have some good friends in the English media, people for whom I have a lot of time. But I never felt that any relationship like that could be established with anyone much from the Australian press. They don't have any qualities I would be interested in. What they write is, in my view, a lot of rubbish.

For example, after the Second Test there was a quote in one of the papers which said that Richards, Ackford and Dooley (all three of us were policemen at the time) did to the Australian team what they do to Pakistanis down on the beat back in England on a Friday or Saturday night. To make a comment like that in a newspaper is outrageous. At one stage we were considering taking legal advice about it. In the end we didn't pursue it because we decided it wasn't a rugby matter and it would be better to let things lie. But it was a shocking thing to write. Through this sort of disgraceful journalism, the Australian media slowly but surely welded us into a strong, cohesive unit which was absolutely determined to win the series. They could not have provided better motivation for us had they done it deliberately.

When you are on tour and everyone seems to be against you, you retreat into a kind of shell into which only your team-mates are allowed. By doing so you create a tough outer skin which anyone tapping from the outside would find very hard to penetrate. We decided we weren't going to take anything from anybody. And we formulated a plan before the Second Test to deal with any nonsense the Australians might start in the form of physical intimidation. This was something which had worked for Willie John McBride's 1974 Lions in South Africa; they had defended themselves collectively against any assault on an individual Lions player.

Rugby is a tough old game. You get a lot of different kinds of people playing it and one or two of them will go on to a field to test the opposition in a physical sense. They want to see how far they can push opponents and whether they will retaliate. It's almost a sort of ritual; marking out territory and seeing whether you are going to be challenged. Given that, I cannot for a moment accept the opinion of the Wallaby coach Bob Dwyer, who subsequently wrote in his autobiography, *The Winning Way*: 'The Lions who toured Australia in 1989 were at times the dirtiest team I have ever seen in international rugby. I say this because their use of foul tactics was not occasional but was a common and consistent theme of their play. With the Lions dirty play was a persistent, deliberate, all-embracing tactic.' Bob is entitled to his opinion and he is a man I respect for the quality of his sides. But I have to say that I strongly disagree with that. We were hard, tough and extremely determined after losing the First Test, that I don't deny, but we were not a dirty side. I think this is no more than a bit of Aussie whingeing about a series they lost after going one-up in a three-Test contest.

The Australians are not by nature a people to stand back and allow you to impose yourselves on them. They 'front up', as they like to describe it, which means that if you are playing them on the sporting field you have to do the same. That is the only way they will respect you. This was not a dirty tactic with violence as its aim, it represented hard reality. If the opposition did not seek to stir us up and mix it illegally or brutally, then nothing would happen. But if they began any nonsense, we were prepared for it. It was as simple as that. We wouldn't look for a fight – we wanted only to play rugby – but if it came we would all help to sort it out.

We went into the Second Test knowing that it would be very difficult, but we also knew we had a better side than in the First Test. There were five changes from the side which played the opening international, and of the five who came in four were Englishmen. This confirmed that the English style was to be tried now. The arrival of Rob Andrew as a replacement for the unlucky Paul Dean, who had been injured early on in the tour, was to prove one of the most influential changes. Scotland's Craig Chalmers had played at fly-half in the First Test and he is a very accomplished player, but we really needed to know where the ball was going and who was doing what. With so many English players in the pack we had to be aware of where the breakdown was likely to be. With Craig we didn't know what to expect once the ball had been moved out from the breakdown or off first-phase possession. In the Second Test, the link between Rob Andrew and the pack, especially the back row, was altogether clearer and better than it had been with Craig. We could not allow the Wallabies to play in the same way as they had done in the First Test. We had to disrupt them, knock them back hard in the tackle, make sure our own first-up tackles were solid and reliable and give them no space in which to run. And we had to deny them possession.

To be fair to the Australians, all the Wallaby sides I have played against have been relatively clean. Some individuals have overstepped the mark just as some players from most countries have done, but you couldn't say that the Wallabies are a dirty side. Before I first toured there, I'd heard stories about certain Australian guys who had a reputation as hit-men and about how physical, macho and hard the Aussies were. It was only when we got there in 1988 that we found out that rugby nowadays in Australia is a middle-class sport and the hard men mostly play Rugby League. League is a very physical game and you see more cheap shots going in, certainly in Britain, than in Rugby Union. But League players don't get involved in rucks and mauls, nor do they have to do as much work collectively around the field as Union men.

I am sure that the intensity with which we confronted the Australians in that Second Test at Ballymore, Brisbane, shocked them. I didn't know at the time how the fighting started, but unknown to us at the first scrum, Nick Farr-Jones had pushed Robert Jones and Robert had retaliated by standing on his foot. It all spilled over from that. As we had planned beforehand, when the trouble came everybody got stuck in. I don't think the Australians knew what had hit them. They had expected us to just sit back and try to play fancy, open rugby. But by the end of the game they knew they'd been in a battle and they realized that they were facing a team which was fiery, could play rugby and could certainly look after themselves.

Even so, it was a close-run thing. We were still trailing by 12–9, with less than five minutes to go. But Robert Jones' tactical kicking was outstanding and, with the pressure on, we suddenly scored two tries through Gavin Hastings and Jerry Guscott. Jerry had played only one international for England when he made his debut for the Lions in that Test. It's not every player who could handle such instant elevation to the top level, but then Jerry is hardly an everyday sort of player. By chipping through and running on to control the ball and score that crucial try, Jerry instigated the Guscott legend. And what a legend it has turned out to be. He really is some player: he has an eye for the gap; he is one of these people who creates so much time for himself that he never really looks under that much pressure. Whatever he does, it normally has an unmistakable touch of class about it. He is a very lucky chap, because guys like him are born only once in a blue moon.

We had a splendid evening in Brisbane that night after the Second Test. The celebrations went on long into Sunday morning, and funnily enough, we probably drank more beer in that crucial last full week leading up to the deciding Test than we had done on the whole trip. I'm not quite sure why, but things seemed to turn out that way.

One difference between 1989 and the 1993 Lions tour to New Zealand was that in Australia, we didn't have the same number of travelling fans who had come out from the UK. There were the ex-pats, of course, and the back-packers, but not the legions who seemed to make the long trip from Britain to New Zealand four years later. I think that if you are going to have a successful tour you need to isolate yourself from the supporters. You just don't want any interruptions at all. It is probably impossible to be totally secluded, because wherever you go there are always people, fans from home and locals, coming up and asking for autographs and so on. That is only to be expected and is easy to handle. Of course, we do value the support and enthusiasm they put behind us, but I think the tour to Australia benefited from the lack of travelling fans because it meant we could concentrate solely on our rugby. When things turned against us, we could look inwards and build the spirit and togetherness which was eventually to prove decisive.

I know that on paper the last Test was close, 19–18 to us – and that result only came about, so every Australian said afterwards, because David Campese made a howler behind his own line and gift-wrapped a try for Ieuan Evans. But although I can't describe exactly why I felt this, I never thought we were going to do anything other than win that Third Test. I was totally confident that we would come out on top.

Nevertheless, I suppose the game did turn on Campo's mistake. If it had been anyone else, everybody would have felt very sorry for him, but Campo was one of those who had been criticizing us heavily in the papers and giving us a lot of stick. We did feel a certain amount of sympathy, but because it was him, there was definitely a feeling that it couldn't have happened to a more deserving bloke! At least Campo speaks his mind, which is more than some people do. He's what the Australians call a tall poppy – someone who stands out from the crowd and says what he thinks. I have always found him very pleasant personally, but I must admit that at the end of the series a lot of the guys were still smarting over what he had said about us.

That win marked the first overseas series for the Lions in fifteen years and victory was sweet indeed because the character of the side had at last shone through. Much of the credit for that must go to Finlay Calder, who reserved by far his best game of the entire tour for the last Test. By then, Finlay had proved himself a very good leader. The trouble at the start of the tour must have made things very difficult for him. Having played against him on a number of occasions, I knew all about his Scottish pride, but he had to try to change and to gel with the English. He tried to make the best of it even though he found it hard at times, and when I look back on it all I realize what a fine job he did as captain.

The Australians were worthy opponents and had more than capable individual players, but they couldn't match us for fire-power. At the end of the day we wanted to win more than they did. Forwards like Steve Cutler and Bill Campbell were very good line-out jumpers, but when it came down to the nitty-gritty stuff they were nowhere to be seen. The Wallabies lacked an enforcer, someone who was prepared to put his head on the chopping block and get down there and get kicked and hurt. The Lions pack had eight of those; the Australian pack had four or five half-hearted candidates and that was about it.

It had proved to be a triumph of a tour for the Test half-backs, Robert Jones and Rob Andrew. Robert wasn't the type of person who went around spouting about the kind of game we should or shouldn't play. But he was an outstanding scrum-half because if one method wasn't working he would just quietly and calmly change the way things were done during a match. The three players in the positions crucial to the side – fly-half, scrum-half and No. 8 – were all capable of fitting into a game plan and also of playing well together. We were all adaptable, though perhaps Rob was less so. I think with that flexibility we helped to turn things around. Rob certainly played better on that tour than he had at any time before with England. Rob is one of these people with whom you know exactly what he is going to do next. He very rarely makes a break at international level, and if he does he is usually only looking for support. But on that Lions tour he was exactly what we needed, and that brought him into his own and gave him a lot more confidence. He suddenly found himself in a situation he didn't have with England, enjoying that little bit more time because of the strength of the Lions pack and the class of the scrum-half in front of him. Indeed, the series marked the start of the England pack's domination in world rugby.

Off the field, Australia was a nice place to tour, although one incident nearly caused the whole trip to end in tragedy. Some of us went on a whitewater raft down some rapids near Cairns in the north of Queensland when we were up in the north of the state. It was great fun, but unfortunately, one of the boats carrying some of the Lions tipped them out in the rough water. Dai Young hit a rock and was being sucked down by the current. Suddenly, his name seemed as though it might become a tragic prophecy. Luckily for Dai, Mike Teague was near enough to him to be able to grab him and keep his head above water. Mike managed to hold on to him until help arrived and the two of them could be dragged to safety. For a moment, it had looked a desperate situation and they were both shaken up. But as with the tour itself, things came right in the end after some initial unhappiness.

As for Lions tours of the future, I am convinced that Australia is a worthy destination. Some games might have been easier than others, but even if you score forty points in a lowlier fixture, you have had to work hard to get them. But we found an improving standard in several places where we might not have expected it. Western Australia, for example, have a lot of New Zealanders in their side, and then there are Australian Universities and the Australian B side. These were not easy matches for us. There were enough tough matches to more than justify the tour. Besides, I think the days of the long tour are over for good, unless you turn the sport professional and are able to pay players to be on the other side of the world for twelve or sixteen weeks. Unless that radical step is taken, I think five- or six-week tours are here to stay.

On the other hand, I'd say the Australian tours to the UK don't include enough matches in any one country. I would like to see them play some club sides, Bath, Leicester and Wasps perhaps, some divisional sides and also a three-match Test series against one nation. It would be better for both teams to have that. You could certainly sell out Murrayfield or Twickenham three times over to see the Wallabies play a series against Scotland or England, so there are sound commercial reasons for the idea. After seven weeks you start to get a better measure of a touring side, which means that a match between two international sides gives a fairer reflection of which is the stronger. At the moment, a one-off Test has only a limited value to either side.

So the 1989 British Lions returned victorious under a Scottish captain and, as luck would have it, four years later, the next Lions party set out, this time for New Zealand, with another Scot as leader. Perhaps it's the porridge that makes skippers grow on trees north of the border . . .

When the Five Nations season began Will Carling was so far down the road as favourite to lead the Lions that he seemed out of sight. He had been in charge as England won Grand Slams in 1991 and 1992, and although we had not won the title in 1993, there seemed no one else remotely in contention when the International Championship began. However, events began to conspire against Will as the season progressed and England finished poorly, in the middle of the table with two wins but two defeats against Wales in Cardiff and Ireland in Dublin. I still thought Will would get the vote. He had a long experience of leadership and it seemed likely that the overwhelming majority of players selected for the tour would be from England. It seemed to make sense to choose the man who had already led them for England.

Fifteen Englishmen were originally chosen to make the tour, which became sixteen when Martin Johnson replaced Wade Dooley. By contrast, there were just seven Scots, five Welshmen and two Irishmen, although Ireland provided two replacement threequarters. To captain this party on what was sure to be a tough tour, Gavin Hastings of Scotland was picked. Clearly, the Five Nations results did not have a great bearing on the final decision because Scotland finished the Championship level on points with England, again with two wins and two defeats. But one of those failures was a heavy 26–12 loss to England at Twickenham.

At least the Lions selectors had learned one thing from 1989: they chose as captain a guy who looked sure to command his place as first choice in his position. Nevertheless, New Zealand wasn't going to be one of the easiest places to tour and I think we needed someone with a lot of character on and off the field to help us through it. I don't believe that either Gavin or Will were as well equipped as people in the past, Willie John McBride, for example, might have been.

Having said that, I am not certain there was anyone on the tour who would have made a better captain than Gavin, nor was a more suitable candidate left at home. The only person who might have come anywhere close was perhaps Peter Winterbottom. Personally I would have picked him as captain rather than just as a player, but who knows whether that would have been the right decision? Peter was very well respected both on and off the field, and although he was perhaps regarded as a little too quiet in some respects, he could still be quite assertive when he wanted to. And of course he was a very charismatic player, someone the others would have followed anywhere.

I don't want to be unfair to Gavin, and I must say that I couldn't put my finger on any one area where he failed. That he was a great player is beyond dispute, but perhaps in a squad which contained a lot of experienced tourists and some strong drinkers, you needed someone in charge who had been there and seen it all before. Someone who realized what was required of a tour like that. Someone who really understood New Zealand rugby. Peter Winterbottom had that experience because not only had he toured with the 1983 Lions, but he had also played a season in the country some years earlier. I would have chosen him as captain. To me he was the ideal candidate. Not that he would have accepted – I don't think he'd have wanted it.

History will condemn this tour as a failure because the Test series was of course lost. And a hell of a lot of strong words were said about some of the players on the tour, and rightly so in my opinion. Unfortunately, the plain fact was that some of the players selected for the tour showed that they just weren't up to it. They didn't deserve to be in the exalted company we were facing week after week in New Zealand.

Yet again the omission of Jeff Probyn was shown to be a serious mistake. Arguably, it was even worse a blunder than his exclusion in 1989, because halfway through the tour of New Zealand, a loose-head prop had to be converted to tight head. That was the ultimate indictment of the original selection procedure and the decisions taken. To have taken a player like Peter Wright and even Paul Burnell ahead of Probyn was a clear error. I know Peter is a loose head and Paul a tight head, but still Probyn should have gone in preference to Burnell. There was no comparison at all between the two. Probyn was still a strong, determined tight head who could anchor any scrum. On a day when hardly anyone in the England team played well, against Ireland in Dublin on the final day of that season's Five Nations Championship, Probyn had been our best forward. To have left him out and taken every other member of that England pack was shameful. It left you wondering whether personality clashes had come into the equation. Certainly something was badly wrong, and the Lions paid for it when they got to New Zealand. The first requirement on a tour there is to have a solid, secure scrum because the Kiwis are very good scrummagers.

But they ended up pushing us all over the place. In my view, the scrum was never right on the whole tour. I know that Jason Leonard was heroic in switching across from loose to tight head when the crisis was at its worst – indeed, the only time the pressure on our scrum ever eased was when Leonard switched roles – but otherwise, we were always under the cosh there.

One of the chief problems the 1993 Lions faced was insufficient strength of character in the midweek side. A lot of them liked to go out boozing, but then so did the Saturday side. However, when it came down to it, the Saturday players put in the performances on the field. We might not have won the series in the end but we took a Test off the All Blacks and would have won the rubber but for a doubtful refereeing decision in the final minutes of the First Test. The distractions are always there and when things start to go wrong on the field you start to seek out those distractions to take your mind off it. The midweek side began to have problems quite early on in the tour and they got worse and worse as it progressed. Some of the players were just not prepared to accept their responsibilities and dig deep enough or work hard enough to put things right. The social side of the tour simply became too important for some.

Players such as Richard Webster and Mike Teague found themselves very much on their own when they played on a Wednesday, while the likes of Paul Burnell, Peter Wright, Andy Reed and Damian Cronin were found wanting when the shit hit the fan. If I were going into a conflict, I wouldn't put my head on the chopping block and expect them to be there to support me, whereas with players of the heart and calibre of Webster, Teague, Wade Dooley, Martin Johnson and Peter Winterbottom you are talking about a different breed altogether. Basically, it came down to too many errors in the selection of the squad. But I felt most sorry for Teague, Webster, Kenny Milne, who did very well, and Robert Jones, too. They earned our admiration for the stand they offered when others around them were not at the races.

Will Carling was another in that category. When he got dropped from the first team and found himself in the Wednesday side, he admitted that it was just about the first time in his life he had been dropped. But he then went on to play outstandingly and to lead by example. A lot of people expected him to go the other way but he knuckled down. It must have been a hell of a kick up the backside for Will, but when he went into the midweek side he shone. For the final Test, I should think it was touch and go who they picked between Will and Scott Gibbs, but Scott had played so well throughout the tour that they probably had to go with him.

The replacements who came out during the tour were also bad choices. I thought it was unbelievable that Richard Wallace and Vincent Cunningham should receive call-ups when the fact was that neither of them was ever going to be up to the task, and hindsight confirmed my view. In the final midweek match against Waikato, Richard Wallace was put through to score and tripped over a blade of grass or something. There were other players back home who would have done a far better job – Mike Hall of Wales or Phil de Glanville of England, for example – players who were used to a standard of hard rugby week in, week out in their home countries.

You have to remember that village life and local rugby in Ireland is very, very different from the kind of game they play in New Zealand. When these guys got out there they couldn't handle it, just as Peter Wright couldn't handle the scrummaging chores – at one scrumfive, he detached himself to guard the blind side! The fact that barely twelve months after being selected as replacements for the Lions tour neither Cunningham nor Wallace went with Ireland to Australia rather proved my point. They should not have been there; they didn't have the necessary credentials. If you are going to work at the coalface, you need hard men, people who are used to it. Wales do have people who could hold their own in confrontational situations. Their rugby is quite physical, as South Africa found out during their tour of Wales and Scotland in 1994. Australians and New Zealanders, too, have come to discover this in the past.

One Irishman who was hard enough to have done well on this kind of tour was Neil Francis, and perhaps he should have come. I am not saying that Reed and Cronin are soft, but they are not the most physical of players. Future Lions selectors should learn from the mistakes that were made in 1993. When you go to New Zealand to play their tough sides, the very first thing you want and are entitled to expect is a team which is able to compete with them up front and can win its own first-phase ball and contest second-phase possession. I would also have taken two strong men to anchor the scrum – Jeff Probyn and Ireland's Peter Clohessy, who is a very hard and very physical player.

Many people thought Stuart Barnes might seize the chance to take the number one Lions stand-off position but it didn't work out that way. Barnsey is a great lad who likes his beer and wine. He is much more flamboyant than Rob Andrew, but he had a habit of staying out drinking later than might have been advisable when we really needed stability. He always had a great deal to give as an inventive half-back, but sadly, he didn't really offer what we wanted in those circumstances.

The 1993 tour certainly wasn't as pleasurable as the 1989 trip. Everyone got on well enough and there wasn't the Scottish–English conflict we'd had four years earlier, but the fact that some of the Lions didn't put in the wholehearted effort required caused a little animosity to grow up towards them. It's hard to watch guys out partying and drinking until late when you are working your butt off to succeed. This was the sort of situation in which a captain like Peter Winterbottom might have fared better in reining in these blokes than Gavin did. Peter was always widely respected as a player, even by his opponents, and he could perhaps have inspired the others rather more. Gavin did his best, but still the partying went on.

Because at the end of the day, the standard of rugby in New

Zealand is unbelievable. Sides like Waikato and Auckland
would beat many of the world's current international sides. And
remember, this was not widely held to be New Zealand rugby's
finest era.

9 My Police Force Career

I didn't see the shotgun until we got quite close to the bulky outline of the figure in the telephone kiosk. It was sawn off, and sticking up out of the man's coat. Luckily for us, he had his back to my young colleague and me, so the element of surprise was in our favour. I rushed the last few yards to the phone box, threw open the door and pinned the guy against one side of the kiosk with the gun sticking right up in the air. I made sure I kept him there until help arrived.

It was not until some time later that the reality of the situation dawned on me. If the guy had turned round before I got to him and held him, he could have blown the pair of us away. Even when I managed to restrain him, all he would have had to have done was to drop the gun and force his hands on to the trigger and my colleague and I might have been yesterday's heroes. I think it shocked the young bobby I was with.

We had received a call from a woman who said a chap with whom she had allegedly been having an affair was threatening to kill her and her husband. He had gone to this telephone kiosk, rung them up and told them he was armed and was going to shoot both of them. They slammed down the phone and called the police straight away. I was on patrol in the area and got the call, so my colleague and I were the first to arrive. We established later that the gun had indeed been loaded. The trouble is, you never know if someone is going to use it or not.

They say that in many circumstances you just react instinctively and think about it afterwards, and that is what happened to me that night. It was the closest I have ever come to having someone point a gun at me. By then, I had been in the police force for a few years and had a good idea of what to do. I was certainly more prepared than I was when I stumbled upon my first serious incident as a young police recruit.

I joined up on 17 May 1982, soon after my return from France. After a period as a probationary constable and then a three-week spell working with a senior officer who taught me the ropes, I was sent out on my own for a series of night shifts, walking an obscure beat on the outskirts of Hinckley, a residential neighbourhood with a few factories. As I was walking along the road one night, a taxi driver flagged me down and said, 'There's been an accident around the corner.' I jumped into his cab and he gave me a lift there.

A three-wheel Reliant Robin had come around a corner too fast, slid along a wall, hit a lamp post and split into various pieces across the road. The car was on its roof and there were two people trapped inside, one of them groaning. As an 18-year-old bobby with about ten days' experience of work on the beat, I was expected to deal with it all efficiently. So what did I do? I panicked! I went right over the top. I got on the radio to report that I was at a serious accident in Southfields Road, Hinckley, and requested assistance.

'How bad is it?' the station officer asked.

'Very bad,' I assured him, adding for good measure: 'We need the Fire Brigade, the flying squad of paramedics from the hospital, ambulances and officials from the accident investigating team in Leicester.' I imagine the sarge back in the station thought we had something like a sixty-car pile-up with fleets of dead lined up waiting to be ferried to the mortuary.

The first senior police officer who arrived calmly took charge and explained everything that needed to be done in the circumstances. And when enough officers arrived, they just literally ripped the car apart to get at the trapped people. I stood back, astonished. To be fair to myself, it was the first major accident I'd been to. I've attended numerous crashes since, and you do get sufficiently used to them to become calm in handling difficult situations. But in those days I'd never come across anyone injured like that before and it was a bit of a shock to me. Quite a few people had gathered round and, probably sensing that I was inexperienced and didn't really know what to do, they were advising me what to do. Of course, people expect you to be able to work miracles, which of course you can't. If someone's life is in danger, then you plunge in and give mouth-to-mouth resuscitation. But if someone has a broken leg you cannot do much apart from try to comfort him until the ambulancemen come and get a drip in or administer drugs.

I seem to remember that the car driver had been drinking but it was his girlfriend who came off the worst. She was in quite a bad way for a few weeks. Happily, though, they both made a full recovery.

You don't treat every accident in the same way but I certainly learned a lot from watching how the professionals handled that situation. The first thing needed is a cool, accurate assessment of the forces required to deal with the situation, which was my first mistake. Of course, when I got back to the station later, a senior officer took me aside and said, 'OK, it was your first serious accident. But I don't think the flying squad were very amused and the Fire Brigade wasn't really needed. You've got to assess the situation better when you arrive.'

I have now been a police officer for thirteen years, almost twelve of them on the beat attached to Hinckley Police Station. So I have attended many accidents and seen dead bodies pulled out of crashed vehicles, as happened one evening when a woman was involved in a major accident driving home from work. She was killed. I was on the scene as the medical people removed the body. I then had to go to her house, sit down her husband and tell him that his wife was dead. Nothing can prepare you for that. You just have to be as honest and straight as possible without putting it brutally. But if you have to tell a husband that his wife is dead, there isn't very much you can do to soften the blow.

But life in the force is not always about dealing with deadly serious incidents or deaths. There are some funny moments, too. At least, afterwards you have a good laugh about them, though at the time they are anything but amusing. Like the time when a colleague and I attended a robbery at a house – or rather, an attempted robbery which was actually underway outside. Two young blokes had got hold of the owner of the house, an elderly chap, and were trying to force their way inside with him. But the bloke's wife was inside and wouldn't open the door. They told her if she didn't, they'd shoot her husband. She retorted that they'd have to do it, because she wasn't letting them in. Then she telephoned the police.

As we arrived, the would-be burglars saw or heard us and ran off before we realized they were so close, or even still there. But it could have turned nasty for us if we had come by a different route and surprised them. It seemed as though the gun had indeed been a real one.

I began my police career by pounding the beat for two years. I quite enjoyed it, too. A lot of the young bobbies who join up these days are put into a patrol vehicle once they've finished their training, and I don't think this teaches them the communication skills you get by walking the streets. Talking to shop-keepers, residents on housing estates and all kinds of people is invaluable in police work because you become used to dealing with the public and you learn how to gather information. It's all very well going around in a car from one job to another, but it means you miss out on sharpening many of the skills that come with being a bobby on the beat.

I used to get involved with lots of people. I'd kick a football with some kids on a bit of waste ground for a few minutes, and stop to chat with people on my patch. Six weeks later, I might be asking those kids, 'Did you see anyone running round the corner just now?' and the chances are, they'd remember you booting a ball with them and say, 'Yes, he went up that alleyway into number thirty-three.' So I can understand the apparent concern of the general public that nowadays there aren't enough officers on the beat, and that too many are in cars. On the other hand, how many villains these days don't drive? Years ago, there were plenty of criminals who would think nothing of walking two or three miles to do a burglary and then walk back. Now they drive miles to do a job, steal something and then drive off. A bobby on the beat wouldn't be much good chasing a car.

It is very difficult to find a happy medium on this issue. Some people insist that the presence of a bobby on the beat in their area would deter criminals, but frankly I doubt it. If a bobby actually works his beat well and people respond to him, then yes, it can reduce crime, but only to a limited extent. In reality it works only in exceptional cases.

Hinckley is a small community where people tend to know other people's business, and obviously, I am quite well known because of my rugby career. When I'm working I often have to take a look at a few local pubs, which can cause a bit of friction among some of the lads. But at the end of the day it's my job, and I wouldn't have to deal with them if they hadn't done anything wrong. Everyone is different and that goes for criminals as well as the law-abiding. You get the likeable rogues who, when you catch them, say: 'It's a fair cop.' If you see one of them in a pub some time later he might very well buy you a pint and you'll buy him one back – even if you have locked him up. But examples of that type are getting few and far between. I suppose they're of the old school, the old criminal class who by and large accepted their punishment if they got caught and viewed doing their time as an occupational hazard. They didn't come out harbouring grudges. Nowadays, the more obnoxious and rude kind of people tend to predominate.

Serious crime was not unknown to Hinckley, but often, it was just the pub scuffles that you have to take charge of. I remember one which started when a youth sporting a cracking black eye came around a street corner and bumped into me. He told me he'd been beaten up, and as we'd been having problems with a group of people from a local village, we went to the pub they used to investigate. We found a group of five youths there. Two other officers and I had a word with them, and after hearing their side of the story we told them that we were doing them for assault. The police van turned up to take them to the station, but they wouldn't tell me who had hit the guy and the chap himself could not identify his assailant. We knew that it was one of this group, so we started to put them into the van. That's when the trouble began. Someone aimed a punch at me, and as he was bundled into the van his mates joined in. There were five of them, three of us plus the driver, and things got to the stage where a passing ambulanceman had to stop and try to assist us in the mêlée. After a while, we got things under control and took them all off to the local police station.

I've seen some sights in and around pubs in my time, but I've only ever been hit once in a pub fight – and that was by a woman! The pub was on a local housing estate and the fight was well in progress when we got there. We tried to sort it out, lifting one chap off another to take him outside. His wife, however, wasn't at all enamoured with that solution, and she ran over and punched me in the face. I was so embarrassed that I didn't do anything to her – I didn't even arrest her. But I kept hold of her husband and took him out. I think she suddenly realized what she had done, because she ran over to the other side of the room and looked pretty concerned, but I left her there.

We took the guy back to the station and later that night someone asked me, 'Did you get hit in that pub?' Sure enough, I could feel a black eye coming up, but I was far too embarrassed to admit that a woman had whacked me. So I said, 'No, I must have bumped it somehow.' I was too humiliated to tell anybody. She was lucky, because if a bloke had done that, I would almost certainly have run him in. It might appear a bit sexist, but she was saved by my pride!

One night, while I was on duty in one of the local villages, a villain who had recently been released from prison did go for me in quite a big way. We saw him as we drove up the road in the police car and we had to stop because he was trying to push a bicycle in front of the car. I pulled over and asked him what he was doing, and he started shouting and swearing, saying that I had only stopped him because I knew who he was and that he'd just come out of prison. Then he began threatening to wallop me and warmed to his theme. In the end, he said, 'Right, we'll sort it out man to man.' I tried to dissuade him from this course of action but he went ahead and threw a few punches at me, so I had to forcibly restrain him and get him in the back of the police car. He couldn't understand when we got to the station why he'd got so many bumps and bruises and I hadn't got any.

Generally, though, my physical size has probably helped me to avoid confrontations – that and my reputation as a rugby player. When you are 6ft 4ins and around 17½ to 18 stone, you cut a fairly imposing figure. In Hinckley, it helped me being a local lad because often when a fight broke out the guys involved were people I knew. I'd walk in and they'd stop and say hello. But there have been one or two occasions when I've thought my presence or that of another police officer might have made things worse.

We once attended a club where a guy had been threatening people. He had told the landlord of a nearby pub that he didn't like him and that he was going to get a gun. We caught up with him in the local working men's club and he was pretty drunk. We told him we were going to arrest him but as we started to walk out to the police car, he started cutting up. He was almost 19 stone and about 6ft 3ins tall, a very big lad. I jumped on him and started wrestling him to the floor. My colleague came to help, and then one of this guy's mates joined in. In the end, it must have looked like a fight at the OK Corral. People were going over tables, furniture was being smashed, and all the while I was trying to get handcuffs on this guy. At one point I looked up and saw a man standing over me with a chair raised above his head. I thought, this is it, I'm for it. There wasn't much I could do in that position, so I braced myself. But one of my colleagues saw what was about to happen, came flying across the room and was just on the point of hurling himself at this man when the man said, all matter-of-factly, 'It's all right, I'm the steward. I'm just putting the chairs back.'

Back in the fray, someone in the room tried to go for one of my colleagues, who threw him off and sent him crashing against a wall. He struck a fire extinguisher hanging there and it hit him on the head as he slid down the wall. The OK Corral becomes the Keystone Cops . . .

Eventually we controlled and arrested the chap we were after and took him outside. His friend, the fire extinguisher bloke, who by now had a growing lump like an egg on his head, came out and started chasing us down the street. We started the car and drove off back to the police station. A while later, this other guy turned up at the station complaining that we had assaulted him, so we arrested him as well.

Early in my career, the transition from teenager to police officer was a little bit awkward for me. I hadn't exactly lived like a hermit in France and I was not the epitome of a law-abiding citizen. There was nothing too wild, but let's just say I used to go out on a Friday and Saturday night and enjoy myself. I found coming back to England and going to work as a policeman in my local town, and seeing all my friends doing the sort of things I had been doing for the last year, albeit in France, a little difficult. It was hard to understand why so many bobbies got on their high horse over what seemed like unimportant youthful escapades. But as time went on, by meeting more and more of the aggrieved parties, I begun to see the other side of the coin. It helped me to look at such behaviour from the viewpoint of the victim rather than through the eyes of the young lad I still was. Gradually my attitude changed, although it took me a good two years to get fully into the swing of things.

While serious crime was a relative rarity in Hinckley, we did once have a spate of five or six murders within the course of a single year. Normally, one murder a year would be the maximum expected in an area like ours, but one after another occurred in this particular year. The most famous case is that of Caroline Hogg, the little girl from Scotland, whose body was discovered on our patch, just outside Twycross on the A444. She had clearly been dumped from a vehicle, and with the close, fast road links to both the motorway and major A roads from there, it was pretty obvious that we had a wide area to consider.

Caroline was found in the mid-1980s but her murderer was not caught until several years later. Robert Black, a long-distance lorry driver, was arrested on the borders of England and Scotland after he had seized another little girl who was discovered bound and gagged in the back of his vehicle. Receipts for petrol and motorway service-station visits proved that Black had been in our area around the time that Caroline's body was believed to have been dumped, and he was eventually found guilty of her murder, together with that of another child, Susan Maxwell, and others. He received life imprisonment.

At the time of the Caroline Hogg case, I was very young and my only role in the investigation was helping with the spot-checking of cars and drivers after the body was found, so I wasn't that close to it. But people have often asked me what goes through the mind of a police officer, especially one who is married with children, in such circumstances. Because of my peripheral involvement in that case, and because I was single then, I was probably less emotional than I might otherwise have been. Of course, you share everyone's sense of sadness for the family and despair at what sort of person could commit such an act. Something like that must be heartbreaking for the parents. Now, as the father of a young daughter, I honestly don't know how I would react if I were in Caroline's father's shoes, or if I had been the man who found his daughter in the back of Black's lorry. She had been playing in the street and had just been snatched, and someone had seen the lorry drive off. By the time the police arrived the lorry had gone, but suddenly it reappeared at the end of the street. When it was stopped and the driver apprehended, it was the father who climbed in and found his daughter bound and gagged under a pile of rags.

It was said that she had a look of absolute terror on her face.

I don't know how I would handle that situation, whether I would cry for joy that I had found my daughter even though she was in a state, or whether I'd just flip and do something to the guy which I would obviously regret later, but which at the time I would feel was morally justified. I guess you don't know what your reaction would be, either. I just hope neither of us is ever in a position to find out.

Another famous murder around that time was that of an Indian diplomat who had been kidnapped from his home in the Birmingham area. I had just come on night shift, and we had a report of a drunk lying in a farm gateway near one of the villages outside Hinckley. I responded and set off for the scene as back-up for the IRV (Instant Response Vehicle). They got there first, and as I pulled up, the other officer said to me very firmly, 'Don't come near.' The 'drunk' had turned out to be the diplomat. He'd been shot twice in the head.

My biggest concern when I arrived was that the people who had dumped him there might still be around. But again, I had very little to do with this case. With a major incident like that, you find that troops suddenly come from everywhere and take over. I think someone was arrested and charged for the crime soon afterwards.

Cases in which you do have a close involvement, especially those in which you come face to face with death, still get to you, no matter how many years you have been with the force. A couple of years ago, I was called to a house fire where a married couple and their two young children, aged two and four, lived. It was on an estate in a small satellite town just outside Hinckley and my colleague and I got there just before the fire brigade. We were met by neighbours shouting that there were children trapped inside the blazing house. We looked up and saw that all the windows had been blown out by the heat, and flames were coming out of the roof. Someone had put a ladder up to the back window but when we tried, we couldn't even get near the ladder, let alone the window, because the heat was so intense. It wouldn't have mattered what equipment we had, you just couldn't get into the house. We had to stand there and watch it. Everyone inside perished.

In situations like that you feel totally helpless and useless. You wish you could do more. But in those circumstances and given the intensity of the blaze, I don't think anyone could still have been alive even when we first arrived. Knowing that doesn't stop you experiencing a feeling of awful emptiness and sorrow. That day those feelings were then replaced by anger. The people next door started complaining that they weren't allowed into their house to get their things out. The fire brigade were working to try to get the fire under control and these people were concerned with their own possessions. Four people had died in the fire and all they were interested in was their belongings. I found that heartless.

So of course policemen can be emotional, and indeed there is a time and a place for emotion. If you didn't care then you probably wouldn't be in the job in the first place. Things get to you as they do to anybody else – we're all human, after all. But afterwards I think you have to remind yourself that it is just part of the job. It is not very nice, but it is life and it happens. And life, in the broader sense, goes on. It has to.

Policing today is a great deal more difficult than it has ever been before. For a start, the villains have changed. There used to be people around the town who were classed as hard because they could handle themselves with their fists. But nowadays, a hard man is someone who carries a knife (in the eyes of the villains, anyway) or, in some cases, a gun. The behaviour of people when they are arrested is changing all the time. I don't think that stems from any difference in the attitude of the police, but from the fact that people now have so many rights and know about them that when we arrest them, they can basically do as they please when they're inside. The only inconvenience for them is that they are in a cell. They can go into an interview and say, 'No comment,' so unless you've got them bang to rights they'll probably get away with it. They receive coffee and lunches, and the lunches have to be of a certain standard. Some of them are treated a lot better than they would be at home, where money might be short.

All this reflects the changes in society itself. Years ago, local kids used to boot a ball about in a town or on the local field, or they'd read books at home or take part in organized activities like the Scouts. Nowadays, the in thing seems to be hanging around the town with your mates on a weekday night to see what's going on. That inevitably leads to trouble, and the troublemakers are getting younger because parents are not keeping a sufficiently close eye on where their children are going and what they are doing. I know it's difficult, and I haven't yet encountered this problem because my daughter is only two and a half. But when she's fourteen, fifteen or sixteen, I'll be finding out where she's going and with whom. It is my view, and it's only a personal opinion, that parents have a lot to answer for. They don't take enough responsibility for their children.

And of course, sometimes the parents themselves are involved in crime. People say that we are twenty years behind America. If that is true and we inherit all America's social problems, this country is going to have some pretty horrific times ahead of it. I think we are too soft in this country and at some stage in the future I believe we are going to have to come up with a better deterrent for crimes such as terrorist offences and murders. Somewhere along the line there is going to have to be a case for hanging. This, I stress, is my own personal opinion, not that of the police force in general or of my own local constabulary, but a lot of people I have met have expressed a desire for punishments to be more severe than they are at the moment, even if they do not want to see the death sentence brought back. If America does hold a vision of our own future, with more and more states in the USA reintroducing capital punishment, I just wonder how long it will be before it is brought back here as well. Who knows, perhaps in ten years time or so we will be doing the same.

I know people worry about miscarriages of justice, but the

introduction of so many more safeguards in the system, such as videotapes and recordings of all interviews, has greatly reduced the scope for fabricated evidence. In the past some interviews which were supposed to have taken place hadn't done so, but now everything that is said in an interview is there on tape for anyone to hear. Suspects also have many more rights than they used to have.

As a serving policeman, I have no time for any officers, however few and far between they might be, who have changed or fabricated evidence in order to secure a conviction, especially for financial gain. Nothing excuses that, even if you believe that someone is guilty of a horrible crime. If you have put hundreds of hours into a case and know for a fact that you've got the right person for the crime, but what you have got is not quite enough to get a conviction, it can be desperately frustrating. So what do you do? You have to let the suspect walk free. I would, and I am sure that 99.9 per cent of bobbies would, but there are a few officers who would not because they knew the suspect was guilty. I can understand what those officers have done and why, but it is wrong. It is the duty of a police officer either to come up with conclusive evidence that he is willing to put before a court, or to release the suspect. You cannot fabricate evidence.

The commissioner for the Metropolitan Police said in 1995 that some officers were being driven to make up evidence in order to get convictions. The home secretary said that that was never right in any circumstances, or words to that effect, and I agree with him. But there is no doubt that the introduction of the Police and Criminal Evidence Act has made it much more difficult to corrupt the procedure. When you arrest somebody you must either have seen him commit a crime or have reasonable suspicions that he has done so. This stage provides the only opportunity for the fabrication of evidence. From that moment on, from arresting a suspect and taking him to the police station to the interview, everything is on video. So in many ways, this act has done us a lot of good. It has brought to the forefront areas in which we were severely lacking before. Without it people would have got away with many more crimes and there would have been more appeals than is now the case.

But the downside of the act is that it is very restrictive on the police. The worst aspect of this is that it dramatically cuts down the amount of time you can spend out of the station doing your policing where it is wanted – on the streets – because it has generated so much more paperwork. The procedure you have to go through when you go to a police station is now much more time-consuming. You used to be able to take into the station someone who, let us say for the sake of example, had been caught driving while disqualified. The interview would probably have gone something like this:

Q: Were you disqualified?
A: Yes.
Q: Have you got insurance?
A: No.
Q: Were you driving such and such a car at such and such a place at a certain time?
A: Yes.
Q: Do you realize what you were doing was wrong?
A: Yes.

These were basic questions which clarified the situation and proved the offence. Now, however, instead of a quick twenty minutes, you are talking about as long as two hours, even for something as straightforward as this, just because of the procedure. The interviewee is asked whether he wants a solicitor and whether he wants anybody telephoned, the tape machine has to be checked and set, forms have to be filled in and every interview is fully recorded. I'm not saying that this is not a bad thing, but because of the length of time it takes I feel we have moved two steps forward and one back. In big cases, terrorist incidents and murders, for example, this procedure is essential, but surely minor misdemeanours such as road traffic offences could quite easily be dealt with by a short interview without having to go through the whole process of booking somebody in. Perhaps a little more common sense in drawing up the act would have been in order.

I moved over to motorway patrol duty almost two years ago, having spent twelve years at Hinckley, which was probably a little bit too long. In a small town everyone tends to know your business and you know theirs, as I've said, and I wanted a fresh challenge. On the motorway you keep yourself to yourself, which is a nice change for me. It's a job in which I am quite settled at the moment. People often recognize me on the motorway but I never try to use that to my advantage. I'm a policeman, not a rugby player, at work. But being known has its advantages; a chat about rugby for a few minutes can defuse any tension. But you have to be aware of what you are doing at all times. People would be far more likely to report me than PC Plod they didn't know, so I have to ensure that I am always beyond reproach.

Being able to drive fast and safely at the same time is always of paramount importance in this task. Sometimes you see people doing 110 m.p.h. down a motorway with one hand on the wheel and in the other a mobile phone held to their ear. That's not what I would call driving safely. I have to be able to drive at speed to do my job and I am trained for it, but others driving too fast does concern me. The general discipline of drivers in this country, especially in keeping to the correct lanes on a motorway, is terrible. You see so many people driving at 55 or 60 m.p.h. in the middle lane with nothing inside them, causing a huge hold-up behind. If these people took a few moments to think, they might solve a lot of problems by moving over. Our force had a blitz on lane discipline earlier this year and it was thoroughly justified. People who stay out in the middle or off-side lanes cause congestion and frustration to others which can lead to accidents and deaths. They do not realize how important it is to drive in the right lane. Bigger motorways would perhaps ease the congestion but raising driving standards is of the most critical importance. There are so many cars on the road now that problems are often caused simply by the tremendous volume of traffic, but poor driving helps no one.

I wouldn't like to see this country adopt the American and Australian style, which allows overtaking on the nearside as well as the offside. It would become a free-for-all and you just wouldn't know where the cars were coming from. If you had three people all doing 50 m.p.h. in each lane nobody would be able to get by. They wouldn't be doing anything illegal, but they'd be causing even more congestion.

When you drive on a motorway you have to be aware of the dangers. Knowing stopping distances is crucial and can save your life in certain circumstances. General fatigue and the condition of your vehicle can also create risks. It's not just on motorways that you can fall asleep at the wheel, of course, but it is a particular hazard on motorways where there is less to keep you alert.

Balancing the requirements of my job and my sport has proved difficult at times, but I am very fortunate in that the force has always given me time off when I have needed it. I am not the type of person to ask for favours every other week, and I don't ask for buckshee time off because I like to work my hours and I take my job seriously. I use a lot of my annual leave to fit in things like rugby tours. The police have always been very good and understanding about it, and I don't wish to repay that assistance by abusing the system.

I try to save up as much leave as possible from my overtime to keep for short family breaks. I haven't had a lot of holidays with Nicky in recent years, but of course that will change when my rugby career comes to an end. Then I will be able to enjoy family life a lot more than I can now. I once went for a fourteen-day holiday with Nicky in Spain, which, given my lifestyle, was a long break for us. I have never had more than two weeks off and usually it's just seven days. I am not moaning about that, though – I would probably get bored after a week. I like to be active on holiday rather than just lie on a beach – play tennis, go deep-sea fishing, anything like that. I enjoy doing things I don't usually do.

No one, least of all me, is looking for rosettes for giving their time to rugby – if you didn't want to do it, you wouldn't do it – but a little understanding wouldn't go amiss. It is amazing just how little appreciation some RFU administrators have of the amount of time players devote to the game. Until the last couple of years, they had their heads totally in the sand, and I think they still don't fully realize that players aspiring to international level are having to train five or six days a week. Fitting in that kind of commitment around a demanding job is not easy. For an international now, you meet up on a Wednesday morning, which means you must take Wednesday, Thursday, Friday and Saturday off work. Somehow, somewhere you have to make up that time.

I am very grateful to the police for all the help and understanding they have shown. They have been scrupulously fair in what they have given me: I wouldn't have expected a day more or a day less. Other services might give more time off – my England colleagues Tim Rodber, who is in the army, and Rory Underwood (RAF) are examples of this – but if I were in their shoes I would feel guilty. I'd feel that if someone were paying me a wage, I'd want to get there and do my bit for the job and earn my money.

Ambitions in my job? Some say I should go for promotion, but I think the higher up the ladder you go, the further away you get from what real policing is all about. What appeals to me most of all about my job is going out and doing the nitty-gritty, helping people, being there and sorting out problems. It wouldn't suit me to sit in a charge room writing down names on a sheet of paper all day long, and that is probably what I would have to do if I were promoted. So I don't know that I would want to change my role at the moment.

I really enjoy my life and wouldn't change anything I have done. I cannot remember any really grim points, and much of the reason for that is due to rugby. I wouldn't have gone to live in France if it hadn't been for rugby; I certainly wouldn't have travelled the world and met as many people as I have. When you see people who have never left their local village, you realize how lucky you are to have seen around the world. There is someone who lives near us who once went ten or fifteen miles down the road to Leicester when he was a teenager. Apart from that, he's never been out of the village. So I count myself fortunate that I have been able to combine a good job with a wonderful time in rugby.

When I play for either the Leicestershire or the British Police I'm able to enjoy both work and rugby at the same time. It's quite odd playing at that level because you see people with perhaps just as much ability as some first-class players and you wonder why they don't move to a better club and take up the game. Then, all of a sudden, you find the chink in their armour and you understand why they haven't got further. But many of them could be very reasonable players if they worked at it – the raw talent seems to be there. It would just be a matter of improving their weaknesses. The police matches can be good. Sometimes you have an interesting mix of dire players performing alongside internationals – England players of recent times who have played for the police include Wade Dooley and Paul Ackford.

I do enjoy playing for the force and turn out for them when I can. I was due to represent the Leicestershire Constabulary against our Merseyside counterparts just three days after England's Grand Slam showdown with Scotland in 1995. I was perfectly prepared to play, even so soon after the international, but unfortunately I picked up a sprung rib cartilage against the Scots and was sidelined for some weeks. However, sometimes I do worry about the possibility of getting injured in those police games – not through violence, but because players at that level often do not know how to enter a ruck or maul properly and without risk of damage to others. A stray boot can come in, completely unintentionally, and catch you in the wrong place. Consequently, there is a greater chance that you will suffer injury than there is in the higher grade, where players are technically superior.

I do regard it as a bit of a duty to play for the police, but if I didn't enjoy it, I wouldn't do it. I am certainly not put under duress to participate. As with all my rugby, I play it because it is good fun.

10 'A Home Life'

Nicky, my wife, could be easily forgiven if she'd asked, 'What home life?' when looking at the title of this chapter, but I'm sure I'm no different from many men of the 1990s in leading such a busy life. Fitting in the requirements of work and family takes quite a bit of doing before you even consider rugby. And of course, when it comes to rugby there are two quite separate demands – those of my club and those of my country. While all this takes a bit of juggling, I am extremely lucky to be in this position, and no one knows that better than me. To play in the first team of a club as good as Leicester is a great honour; to be chosen fairly consistently for your country is something else. I am aware that legions of young rugby players would give almost anything to be in my boots, and that some people struggle on year after year trying to cope with the conflicting and heavy burdens of job and family, just for a little jam on their bread, in many cases. I am able to play rugby at the top level, have some wonderful times, meet some lovely people and get to travel around Britain, Europe and indeed the world quite often. Only a fool would fail to recognize the tremendous opportunities that offers.

To manage my life, I try to prioritize. First comes my family. Secondly, as a direct link to that, my job has to be next in importance because the latter underpins the former – everyone has mortgages to meet and bills to pay, and regular employment is vital. Third comes rugby – in theory, at least. The reality is that often rugby leapfrogs that pecking order and competes with my work for attention. In 1995, there were probably more England squad meetings than ever before in history. We had frequent training sessions at Marlow Rugby Club in the Buckinghamshire countryside. It took me a good hour and a half to get down there on a Tuesday evening for practice, and after a hard, physical programme, you then have, of course, the drive home.

I live within ten minutes of the M1 in Leicestershire and I wish I had a penny for every time I've been up and down that motorway in the last few years, not only with my job, but also for my rugby commitments. If I did, I would be just about able to retire by now. I don't mind the travelling, but I couldn't do it for ever. It is just a necessary part of this phase of my life and I am fortunate that Nicky understands that. My rugby career is finite and in a year or two I expect to have a little more time on my hands.

Since we had our first child, Jessica, I have found myself focusing even harder on my priorities. Before I was married, and certainly before we became parents, I'd sometimes finish a shift with the police at 2 p.m., go off for a game of squash with a friend or colleague and get home around 5 p.m. Nowadays when I finish at 2 p.m., I like to be straight off home to the family, particularly if I have to go down to London the next day for a training session or England squad meeting, even if I can fit in only an hour or two with Nicky and Jessica. I want to spend as much time with them as possible, and going off to pursue your own hobbies does conflict with family life.

When I do find time for outside interests, I like any sport that requires a winner and a loser. I have a strong competitive instinct and that is what motivates me ultimately. I don't play as much squash as I used to but I play a little tennis in the summer. I like golf, too, but I find it very frustrating – I am not one of the best co-ordinated people in the world, and although I hit the ball a long way it does not necessarily go in the right direction. I tend to play one brilliant shot followed by twenty bad ones. Golf is also very time-consuming, and when you hit the ball as badly as I do, it can take as long as four hours to get round the course. My family brings me more pleasure than anything else, so given the choice between a game of squash or perhaps golf and an afternoon with Nicky and Jessica, I'll always favour the latter.

It has to be said that I have started to resent the time rugby demands because it is dragging me away from where I want to be. It is different if you are away a lot through your work – earning a living is a fact of life, and if you have a job these days you are grateful for it. I don't envy some of the boys coming through in rugby, because if the sport does become professional, they will find it extremely difficult if not impossible to handle it all. It will fall to the clubs to create some time for players in the future. We cannot continue to ask so much of people who are receiving absolutely no compensation from the game – the two visions simply do not mix in the modern world. At the moment, a League programme of home and away matches just adds up to too much. I can see that clubs could use the extra revenue, but they have to consider the toll it will take on the players. Rugby is a game of such physical intensity that you cannot play it too often, and to have had home and away League fixtures in 1994–5 with the World Cup at the end of the season was asking the impossible of England's leading players. Even those just turning out for their clubs found the pressures mounting up; for international players it was too much.

I met Nicky at school, the John Cleveland College. We used to pass the time of day during our schooldays, and then met socially as we got a bit older. I don't know if it would be accurate to say that we spent three years courting, because for part of that time I was in France, but even then she was very much on my mind.

We live about twenty minutes' drive away from where I am stationed with the police, and just about the same distance from Leicester Rugby Club. It is close enough to be convenient but far enough away to give me a breathing space from both work and rugby. I have played at Leicester since 1982 and have

devoted a lot of time to the club. If I lived any closer to it I fear
that I would be dragged into even more events and duties. I
certainly wouldn't want to get into the habit of drifting down
to the club for a few pints most evenings. The club would then
become my family and I'd rarely spend any time at home, and
that's not the way I want my life to be. There is only so much
you can give and I don't want to be drawn into the trap of
always being at the rugby club if I am not actually at work at
the police station. I'm sure people will understand that wish.
Plenty of others involved with the Tigers travel even further to
get to the club.

Ours is a lovely, small midlands farming village, surrounded
by farms and fields. The people are very friendly and I don't
feel any urge to move. Not a great deal happens here and we
like it like that. If we want nightlife, we can go to some of the
social events at the club or go into Leicester, a comfortable
drive away, but out here you can find peace and quiet and that
is something of increasing value to us. When I have finished a
shift or a match or have just been training, I welcome the chance
to wind down in the car on the way home. Far be it for a police
officer to say that he switches off at the wheel, but you can
relax even while you are still concentrating on your driving. I
can do my thinking about rugby or the job so that by the time
I get home I can open the door and talk about the things my
wife wants to discuss. I find that quite therapeutic.

I usually train at Leicester on Tuesday and Thursday
evenings. I go to most training sessions, especially in the last
couple of years: as captain, I feel it is essential that I set a good
example by being there as often as I can. There is the odd
occasion when I just cannot get there due to police duties, or
– very rarely – when I have given in to that feeling of tiredness
or complete mental fatigue and not gone, but I don't miss many
training nights. If I had a family problem I would cry off, but
that doesn't happen very often.

One aspect of rugby fame about which I am not enthusiastic
is the pressure the media can apply. Not many people have my

home telephone number and I like to keep it that way. I find it intrusive if journalists telephone me at home. I try to keep my private life private, and there is nothing worse than sitting down to Sunday lunch with your family only for someone to ring up wanting an interview. I accept that the press have a job to do, but they have to look at it from our point of view. Sunday is often the only day when a rugby player is at home with his family. The last thing he wants is to be bothered by endless questions about matches or other events. I regard Sunday as 'my' time and I try to guard it jealously. Unlike some of the other England players, I don't have a newspaper column because I want to be consistent about this. I don't think you can complain about intrusions from some journalists when you are discussing events with another one for a first-person column.

Living in the country with lots of farms nearby makes it easier for me to indulge in one of my great passions: shooting. I like rough shooting – pheasants, rabbits, pigeons, ducks, geese, that kind of thing. The feeling you have when you are out tramping the fields is like no other. You are close to nature, alone or with a couple of close friends, and you feel as if you have gone back to your roots. Like so many other sports, it tends to take quite a bit of time – anything from three to six hours – but at least I don't have to drive for miles before I start like I might have to do to find, say, a suitable golf course. Shooting I can practically do on my own doorstep. I simply love it, even when I don't bag anything and return home empty-handed. You have been out in the fresh, clear country air for some hours and there is nothing better than that. You can think your own thoughts and do what you want to do, go where you want to go. It is freedom. And on the good days, when you do find some prey, you can keep the freezer stocked up as well.

I agree with Ian Botham, who once said that he only shoots things he will later eat. If I shot creatures I knew wouldn't end up on the dinner table, I would probably feel differently about it, but as it is, you are really only another part of the food-chain system. All animals eat other animals, and man is no different.

At the same time, I respect the opinions of those who are against shooting and field sports of any kind. I wouldn't seek to prevent them airing their views publicly and, within reason, going where they want to go to do it. But equally, they must accept that those of us who do love shooting also have the right to do what we want. I do not see the need for confrontation.

I do find both fox hunting and hare coursing unacceptable. When the animal has finally died in those circumstances, no one eats it. If you shoot, you are shooting to eat. To me, it's no different from going to your local supermarket and buying a joint of beef or a chicken off the counter. A chicken is kept in a tiny hut somewhere, whereas the birds I shoot spend their entire lives out in the open.

I have tried clay-pigeon shooting but found it a little too predictable for my taste. That is not to say I am such a crack shot that I find it too easy – far from it. I just prefer the challenge of man against animal in the wild. It seems to me an historic duel that has been carried on down the centuries.

Of course, most of the season is in the autumn and winter, which makes it a bit difficult time-wise, but I do some pigeon shooting in the summer. I was introduced to the sport about seven or eight years ago by one of my police colleagues. Being out there away from motorways, cars, offices, people and houses seemed wonderful to me. Not surprisingly, I didn't shoot anything that first time and there are still many occasions when I don't get anything. I am a better shot than I was in those days but sometimes the birds just aren't there. Maybe they have a sixth sense, I don't know.

I would say that nowadays shooting probably rivals rugby in terms of the pleasure I get out of it. In fact shooting has one distinct advantage: it is one thing I won't be forced to give up in eighteen months or so just because my old bones are starting to complain too much at the physical exertion. I go shooting as often as Nicky lets me – usually once or twice a week. If I am on a police shift which begins at, say, 2 p.m. I will get up early and go out first. A local farmer lets me shoot on his land a few miles from our house. He has a particular problem with rabbits and pigeons and is keen to keep their numbers down, so as well as enjoying myself I am also lending him a hand. Rabbits make a lovely pie and I don't mind skinning and dressing them at home. They need to hang for a while before they are dressed, but they do taste good when cooked. I tend to feed the pigeons to our dogs, although sometimes we eat pigeon pie. I dress other birds, too, such as geese or duck. I think that eating these wild game birds is a great deal healthier for you. They have lived as nature intended and must be altogether better for you than animals which have been artificially fattened by drugs in a restricted area. The culinary horizons of a lot of people extend only as far as roast beef, fish and chips and perhaps a bit of lamb on Sundays. They never try things like goose, partridge, different types of duck. Until you have actually tried a wild goose you don't know a goose at all – everyone has this idea that goose is very fatty, but a wild one isn't at all. It is very pleasant and the meat is quite lean.

From our house we can see open fields and there is room for our two dogs to have a good run. I helped build the house – in fact its construction was a real Leicester family affair. Darren Garforth, our prop forward, provided the scaffolding; Ian Bates, our centre, was the chippy and Tom Smith, who plays in our second row, was the brickie. It was terrific to be able to plan the house ourselves because of course it meant that we could build it the way we wanted it. The downside was that it took a long time to get through all the planning stages and the building, when that finally began. You do wonder after a while whether you will ever live to see the whole project finished! We were eventually able to move in in 1992, about a year after buying the land. By doing the job ourselves and with the considerable assistance of our friends, we reckon we probably saved around forty thousand pounds.

While the house was being built we were living with my parents ten miles away, which necessitated a lot of travelling to and fro. If we ever did the same thing again I think we both feel we would live locally in a rented house or hire a mobile home and live on the site. It would be a great deal easier. I can do a certain amount of work myself but I get frustrated because I can by no means do everything I'd like to do. I tiled the floors and fitted the kitchen and things like that, and I slapped lots of paint around the place too, but not much else. If I'd got involved in the structural stuff, the house might have come down around us by now!

I don't imagine we will be rushing away from this house because we like it so much in this village. When I do finally retire from rugby, whenever that is, I hope to find a little more time to put into doing odd jobs around the house. At the moment, they tend to get put off time and again.

On the subject of retirement, I confess that, like a lot of other players a year or two ago, I probably envisaged the 1995 World Cup as a logical high point at which to end my career, certainly as far as international rugby was concerned. By the 1995 tournament, I had been playing for England for nine years, although injuries meant that I had by no means played an international every season.

Now, however, I am not so sure. I am increasingly aware of the unhappiness I would experience if I retired prematurely. I imagine there is nothing worse in international sport, whatever your game, than to look back on your own playing career with the feeling that you gave up too soon. It is the oldest cliché in the world that you are retired a long time, but it is certainly true. I do not want to make that mistake, and so I decided before I set out for the World Cup that I would postpone a decision until the dust had settled on the competition and I was back home and able to reflect without too much emotion on it all. Since then, I have decided to play on.

The long visits overseas become increasingly hard when you have a wife and child at home. And when I do finally retire, I expect I will be like a lot of players in that I shall want a spell away from rugby doing completely different things. I have noticed that happening to quite a few players. Often, they come back to the game a couple of years later, ready and willing to serve their club, but they need that break to refresh their batteries. I expect to be the same.

I cannot see myself ever giving the kind of time and commitment that people like Geoff Cooke, Dick Best or Jack Rowell have brought to England. It seems almost a full-time job, and I simply could not spare so much time. But I do want to take my coaching certificate so that I can perhaps put something back into my club. I cannot imagine not being involved in the game in some capacity in the future, although I have to say I'm not sure whether I am cut out to be a coach. I don't like watching from the sidelines, and I imagine I'd find it desperately difficult to overcome that. Having to watch others decide your fate with their own successes or failures is far from ideal.

Although you never know what the future will hold, of course, I cannot imagine ever walking right away from rugby and not doing something to help Leicester. Apart from anything else, I would miss the many friendships I have established over so many years, especially at Welford Road. The people there are marvellous and I, like so many other folk associated with rugby, will always be grateful to the game for offering such friendships. I hope they last a lifetime.

11 Rugby's Future?

The date is Saturday 23 January 2010, and there is high excitement at the headquarters of English rugby. Twickenham is preparing for the grand opening of its new upper tier which surrounds the whole ground. For two or three years, spectators have had to put up with some soakings as the roof had to be removed to make way for the new tier of the wraparound stand, but now the work is over and the new capacity of 110,000 will be completely filled for the first time.

No wonder, either. The French are in England today, admitting publicly that they are absolutely desperate to end their nightmare run of twenty-four consecutive defeats in the Five Nations tournament. They haven't won against England at Twickenham since 1987, twenty-three long years ago. The couple of World Cup defeats they also suffered against us, the most recent in the final of the 2007 tournament at Twickenham, served only to heighten their frustration. On the back of that triumph, the Rugby Football Union immediately announced plans to raise the capacity at Twickenham. Three years later the job is done. It all looks superb, but everyone is far from happy. It is still just about impossible for the ordinary punter to get his hands on a pair of tickets. Some blame the continuing influence of the recently retired Lord Burton of Bourton (on the whisky, not water) for continuing to control the ticket allocation for the RFU. Some say things will never change until Lord Burto, as he is fondly known, finally relinquishes all control.

The French arrived in England yesterday afternoon on the recently completed Channel Tunnel rail link which now boasts a fast line all the way from Paris to London. For the first fourteen years of the link, the construction of the fast track from London to the English coast was delayed by the efforts of the last of the lingering protesters, led by the well-known former England coach Lord Best of Stoop, who has campaigned against the rail link since buying a country mansion in Kent some years ago. The French arrived complaining that they had not even had time to finish their oysters, frogs legs and white wine before the flying train began its approach to St Pancras station in London.

Nowadays, though, Twickenham is run and populated by some very famous names from the past. Dudley Wood, longtime secretary of the RFU many moons ago, is halfway through his fixed five-year term as president and is immortalized in a huge bronze statue erected just inside the main concourse at Twickenham. Dudley's nephew is the present secretary. Dudley was brought back to serve in the highest office due to the concern of the RFU committee, who felt that the average age of its members had fallen too low. As a consequence, some of the under-50-year-olds who had only recently been appointed to the committee, including the Rt Hon. W. D. C. Carling, MP, OBE, KG and minister for food, is to be replaced in a shock move against youth by a 175-year-old from the shires, the Lord Michael Bodger of Steele. Others of Carling's era are also to lose their jobs to representatives with ages ranging from seventy-five to eighty-three.

The Rt Hon. William Carling is one man whom you rarely see at Twickenham on big match days. Since his retirement from the playing side some years ago, Carling has retreated to his good-sized house in the suburbs, together with his wife and three children, venturing to Twickenham only for committee meetings – until recently, that is. He has become known as Mr Average, a nickname which seems to delight him. This may be due to the fact that until he finished playing, he never knew what solitude meant. When I bumped into him at a recent RFU committee meeting before his sacking, he confessed that he was forty before he knew what it was to go down to his local pub with a couple of mates and have a few quiet beers without being bothered. I wish him well – he deserves it, because he virtually said goodbye to the first fifteen or twenty years of his social life.

At Twickenham, two hours prior to kick-off, the chief executive of the Rugby Football Union steps out of his sponsored chauffeur-driven Bentley in the official car park. The sight of the advertising slogans down the side of the chief executive's official car bemuses many of the old school who still limp arthritically to Twickenham for the big games. Some of these old chaps are known to be deeply unhappy at the views of a newly elected RFU committee colleague, Mr Brian Moore QC. Brian, a committee man at heart, has always nurtured a cherished wish to become a senior committee member at Twickenham. Since achieving that ambition, he has, alas, caused innumerable problems for the old diehards alongside him.

Of course, the media now plays a hugely significant role in rugby. Television revenue, which has long since run into millions, has enabled England's top clubs to become professional. And talking of TV, thanks to the televising of top legal proceedings, Brian Moore, now approaching fifty, can be seen regularly by the viewing public when he appears in court to represent clients libelled on TV rugby programmes. Moore is a highly sought-after man among the countless rugby players who are suing television companies and newspapers for libel in critical articles written about them.

In other branches of the media, the very, very red-nosed gentleman you may be able to spot behind the perspex glass in one of the individual centrally heated press boxes is the *Daily Telegraph*'s esteemed correspondent. Some will remember him from his playing days. Mr Stuart Barnes, now also a world expert on red wine, is highly respected in his field and also a vice-chancellor of Oxford University in his spare time.

Alas, not all developments in the game are a success story. *Rugby Special* is still not very special, despite having once again fought off rival bids to produce the programme. The favourite to take over, a Dutch TV company, fell out of the running for the contract when it was revealed that it produced hard-core porn movies for pay television in the Netherlands and other parts of Europe. It is alleged, but strongly denied, that certain senior RFU committee members had agreed the deal on the basis of free subscription to all programmes put out by the Dutch company. Meanwhile, the player with the most grotesque cauliflower ears in all rugby, Mr Price of Wales, has been appointed the new presenter of the programme. It is said to be a gimmick.

Speaking personally, I am only too happy to admit that the game has treated me very well indeed since my retirement from the playing side. Until recently, I was first-team coach at Leicester, where I could be seen walking up and down the touchline wearing my sponsored winter coat and tracksuit together with its sponsor's badges down each arm of the jacket. I am equally happy to confirm that the role has made me a very rich man, for of course all coaches at senior clubs have long since been paid in English rugby. I only wish that my other job in the police force had gone as well. Alas, I have to admit that I have graduated from a traffic policeman to a traffic warden.

Many of England's finest players are also receiving handsome financial rewards, especially those who have kept their jobs as well as being paid by their clubs. The top men now take a week off work to prepare for the major internationals. They are easily able to afford time off through their rugby earnings, which run to around five hundred thousand pounds a year for the most famous. Much of this money has come from the huge TV deals which now include a clause paying a percentage to each international player. So professional has it become that England's star men now take their own personal dietician, physio and hair stylist away with them on trips to Five Nations games in places like Paris and Dublin. But only very rarely do their 'assistants' go to Cardiff and Edinburgh – none of them can be persuaded to attend those match weekends, even for an increased fee.

Club rugby has been transformed by the European Club League, which started up some years ago. TV deals for exclusive rights were huge, and now the BBC Sports channel, which costs approximately a thousand pounds a year, televises live a major rugby club match in Europe on several Wednesday nights during the season. Some of the most recent games seen included a cracking match between Agen and Leicester which, as Tigers coach, I was delighted to be able to watch at first hand on a mild night in the south of France. I was also thrilled that a Leicester player won the Man of the Match award, a brand-new motor car from one of the sponsoring companies. Another fine game in the last few months was Harlequins' victory over the Italian champions Milan (complete with the captains of Australia and New Zealand respectively in their side) at a floodlit Twickenham, and the great Bath–Llanelli game, which the English side narrowly won.

But the real rewards for the players will come at the annual challenge match between the eventual champions of the European League and the winners of the southern hemisphere's equivalent competition. Last season's match grossed millions of pounds when the South African provincial side Transvaal met Cardiff, the reigning European champions, before a sell-out crowd of 95,000 at Twickenham. Cardiff had won the northern hemisphere's European League by beating Bath in the final at Murrayfield.

The concept of the European League brought many millions of sponsors' money flooding into the game. And profits from gates are also good because all the early rounds of the European tournaments are played on a home-and-away basis. Then both the quarter-finals and semi-finals are also played over two legs, so the potential for revenue at these matches has become enormous. Indeed, such are the riches to be had nowadays that the seven million pounds paid by Courage back in the 1990s to sponsor matches in the English League alone seems almost comical in its moderation. Mercedes, sponsors of the European League, agreed a seven-hundred-and-fifty-million-pound exclusive sponsorship deal for a three-year term. Players are handsomely rewarded, with lucrative win bonuses now commonplace.

Club rugby has been transformed by the abolition of all the old Draconian amateur laws. It was reported last week that players in the Midlands League Division 1 are threatening strike action unless they receive improved win bonus payments. A spokesman for the players said: 'We just cannot survive on the pitiful few hundred pounds the clubs in this league are prepared to pay their individual players for a win bonus.' The players also want a new, improved package in their renegotiated contracts with their clubs to include a guaranteed signing-on fee when they transfer and shares in the new club's limited company.

Transfer rumours suggest that English rugby's greatest star, the Bath centre Terry Scott, is about to be transferred to the Italian giants Milan in a three-million-pound deal. Scott is said to be receiving a 10 per cent signing-on fee, a sponsored Rolls Royce with a chauffeur for three years, plus a share option in his new club and a five-year contract reputedly worth a million pounds a year.

The 'new Dean Richards' of 2010, known as 'Beano' at Leicester, is to transfer to Orrell for one million pounds and a share in the business which owns the Orrell club. It is involved in the selling of pies, principally in nearby Wigan, where there was once a well-known Rugby League club before the advent of professionalism in Rugby Union hastened its sad demise.

The trend towards players no longer working or only doing so if they wished was heralded by the influx of Australian and New Zealand rugby players into Italian rugby several years ago. A test case in the European court followed soon after, and when judgement went in favour of the applicant from an English club who demanded a similar financial deal, the game changed for ever. But much good has come from the situation. Injured players can now go away for two or even three weeks' rest and recuperation at a series of plush health centres dotted across Europe. It is said that the leading French players even visit the French West Indies and, for the most serious cases, Tahiti, for treatment.

These days, of course, players switch hemispheres at will and, again speaking personally, I do not believe the game has been damaged in any way by this popular trend. It is great to see the top Australian centres Coren and Large playing at Bath together, and their English colleagues at the club insist that the pair have helped to dramatically improve the skills of the other threequarters at the club. It is because the Australians have done so well that Bath can afford to release Scott, thereby recouping some of the tremendous outlay spent on bringing the Australians to England.

My own club, Leicester, sadly cannot boast two such superb backs as Coren and Large but we are very pleased with our Aussie, the fly-half Lineman, who joined us this season. He has helped enormously in developing the youngsters, and to fill our thirty-thousand-capacity stadium most weeks for the major games. Lineman, who plays for the Randwick club in Sydney, joined us because of the tie-up between Leicester and Randwick, a concept which became popular and widespread in English rugby around 2005. It followed a twentieth-century tradition whereby certain towns around the world 'twinned' with others in different countries. The Leicester players who spent the winter months of May to September in Australian club rugby with Randwick had a wonderful time and returned far better players for the experience.

Foreign players have added a lot to the English domestic game and I cannot now see a time when our clubs would not include one or two leading overseas players. Indeed, the sponsors may well no longer pour millions into the major clubs unless they have signed up some world stars. Strangely enough, few New Zealanders are sought after as overseas recruits nowadays. Leicester had one, many years ago, a chap called Stuart Loe,

who was the cousin, I think, of an old New Zealand international prop called Richard Loe. But Stuart Loe never really
settled at Leicester and drifted back to Kiwi-land after a while.
I think he may have missed seeing the sheep. And he never
seemed to get used to the players at our club always visiting
some curry house either in our city or around the country.

Quite recently, after my retirement as coach, I was standing
on the terraces at Leicester's superb new stadium, chanting
'Beano! Beano!', when an elderly gentleman tugged my sleeve.
'I remember you when you played,' he said. 'You weren't a bad
prop. It is Stuart Redfern, isn't it?'

Believe me, you are very easily forgotten in this game. I went
to a local school recently with one of Leicester's former coaches,
Paul Dodge, who also represented England and the British Lions
as a player. The kids knew me because I was still Leicester's
coach, but after they had asked me for my autograph, I said:
'You ought to ask the chap over there for his. He's Paul Dodge.'

'Paul who?' they asked. Enough said, really.

Another former England rugby star, Jerry Guscott, is now a
household name with his own TV programme. Jerry hosts the
long-running *Gladiators*, and has become the new Desmond
Lynam of broadcasting. One of Jerry's old Bath and England
colleagues, Victor Ubogu, is head of a security company which
has expanded so much that it now takes charge of all security at
Twickenham. Victor's company also owns a string of nightclubs
around Britain and abroad, in places such as New York,
Johannesburg, Paris and Rome. Victor flies the world to keep
his hands on the business operation and is met at each airport
by one of the company's many stretch limos. All are for the
personal use of Victor, the chief executive. He is a familiar sight
in the back of the limo, large cigar between his lips, glass of
whisky in one hand and a copy of the *Financial Times* in the
other. He is, of course, a millionaire many times over nowadays.

Rory Underwood, one of my former playing chums from the
old days at Leicester, left the RAF some years ago and now flies
long-haul planes for British Airways. His brother Tony, whom

some will also remember, has done very well in the City, working as a Eurobond dealer.

The new chairman of the Sports Council, Sir Robert Andrew, is another chap I used to know quite well. Squeaky, as he was always known by his playing chums, is also managing director of an internationally known property management company with offices around the globe. In the fifteen years since his retirement, Squeaky has carefully trodden the right path with the right people. He has never contradicted anything those in authority have said and, as a consequence, he is highly respected in business circles. He has been offered many times a safe seat in Parliament with the promise of a ministerial portfolio, but until now, he has been too busy with his private business to accept. Nevertheless, some say that he could well become a future prime minister, with the present minister for food as deputy leader and chancellor of the exchequer.

I like to meet up with some of my old playing colleagues from the good old days. I saw Kyran Bracken recently and was astonished to see that he scarcely had a hair left on his head. Some say it was all the worry over which girl he should finally settle down with that caused the dramatic hair loss. But Kyran has done well in business and is now a big noise in the City.

Tim Rodber, the brigadier, reached high office in the services before taking early retirement. Martin Bayfield is now a superintendent in the Bedfordshire Constabulary and Martin Johnson is a branch manager for the Midland Bank in Leicestershire.

As for myself, I have only one ambition left really. Now that I have made so much money from the sport I have always loved, I plan to buy a country estate, perhaps somewhere in Gloucestershire near King Charles and Queen Camilla's country home, so that I can indulge my sporting hobby of shooting. Gamekeeper is the job I want, on a part-time basis, so that I can spend more time out in the air. My daughter and three sons are all keen country sports followers in the making.

I cannot deny that rugby has provided a wonderful life for me and for the modern-day rugby player in 2010.

Index